# Goal Ripple

To learn more, please visit - GoalRipple.com.

*Coming soon from Adam M. Brest, a complete library of Sales Training, Team Motivation, and Goal Alignment tools and materials to help your business grow and inspire you to achieve your goals.*

# "Who Made these Stupid Rules?"

*The 'Typically A-Typical' view of*

*Life, Business, Sales, Motivation & Goals*

## Adam M. Brest

(Copyright - 2016)

*GoalRipple.com*

## *Dedication:*

This book is dedicated first and foremost to my beloved wife Suzi. You will never know how special you are to me - through all of life's obstacles, your faith in me, your caring smile, and the unbelievable way that you've put up with me for so many years now have meant so much to me. You are my rock, my best friend, my world.

This book is also dedicated to my family and the people in my life I've worked closely with, taught me different points of view, and provided so many laughs along the way. Even in times when we were unsure of how we would achieve our goals, the confidence you placed in me have made me who I am today. The world might curse you for that…. However, I thank you from the bottom of my heart.

# Table of Contents:

Prologue:

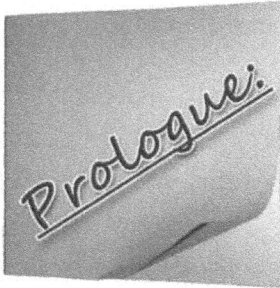

# Hiking the
# "Trail of Fear"

The word "Fear" is used frequently these days. There is something so ominous and inherently evil sounding about it. Like a masked marauder lurking in the bushes waiting to rob a stage coach of weary travelers. You might even say merely hearing the word "Fear" is scary. President Roosevelt famously said "The only thing we have to fear...is fear itself" in his 1933 Inaugural Address to our weary nation during times of turmoil and uncertainty. Allow yourself to daydream for a few moments with me. *By all means, keep reading and stay focused, but allow an open mind to ponder a new possibility.*

I've thought a lot about fear recently. Not for any other reason than I've encountered so many people during the process of writing my book who struggle with fears, both real and imagined.

I have been filled with a sense of wonder and amazement while discussing their viewpoints, hearing their stories, gleaning insight and listening to their concerns. I decided to look inward to learn how I viewed my own fears, both real and imagined. Are they really fears or are they concerns? Perception is a funny thing...

First off, allow me to say *(this will be no surprise to those who know me well)*, I am a worrier. I worry about every little detail. I try to cover all my bases and anticipate every situation. Although you can never make everyone happy, I try to never be the cause of issues. I've been in sales too long and it's just who I am. But I realized that I don't truly fear anything. ***That thought troubled me***. People with no fear are the people who jump out of airplanes with no parachutes. As I began to write down my thoughts, I began to discover how I viewed fear. I've decided that "Fear" is a backpack we carry on our journey. The important distinction is how we fill it and how heavy it becomes...

To this end, I'm taking you all on a hiking trip. Let's grab our bags and begin our trek. "Where are we going?" you ask. "We are hiking the Trail of Fear." *(Cue ominous music)*. We are heading out into the great unknown. But don't worry; we can re-pack our backpacks together.

What do you fear in life? What are you carrying with you? What do you take and what can we leave behind? Think about that for a moment... *It's important to remember that some people are carrying feathers in their pack and some are carrying lead in the same size pack. Size isn't important. The weight is... And it isn't always visible to the casual observer...*

In this book, we will discuss "asking the right questions" when removing obstacles and objections. In my quest to define "Fear", I discovered that most people have difficulty defining their "Fears" just as I did.  Let's look at a few typical fears: the fear of snakes, the fear of heights, the fear of trying, and the fear of failing *(and yes...the fear of failing and the fear of trying are two completely separate things)*. There are also relationship/life fears of being alone, not being accepted, and the fear of leaving or staying in a relationship.

But are we asking the right questions here? What do you truly fear about spiders/snakes? Do you fear the snake or are you simply concerned about being bitten by a venomous species? Now that's an interesting thought.. Is it a giant fear or a minor concern? When we stop focusing on the giant task of "Conquering your Fears" or "Overcoming your Fears", we can begin to simply address the minor concerns that culminate to cause them. Let's work to turn the lead weights of a "Fear" into a few feathers of concern to address.

Do you truly fear heights or do you fear the landing? The joke response we've all heard is to say "I'm not scared of heights, I'm afraid of falling." Are you sure you aren't merely concerned about the landing? The way to answer this is to ask yourself, "how high is too high?" What thought pops into your head? Is the answer "high enough that I would be injured when I landed"? If you were guaranteed to land softly, would you still fear heights?

When we step back, ask the right questions, and truly think about it, we find that most of what we "Fear" is a combination of minor concerns that weigh down our backpacks - 10 lbs of Fear of Heights, 15 lbs of Fear of Poison Ivy, 8 lbs of Fear of Snakes, etc. What are you carrying along with you in your pack? What is weighing you down?

Allow me to give you an example to start repacking our Backpacks for the Trail of Fear metaphor.  I am clumsy. I fall down a lot more than an adult should *(My family and friends are chuckling and nodding their heads)*. I'm concerned about injuries from impact. But I'm also concerned about venomous snake bites on the trail. So how do we address these concerns? How can I lighten the load in my pack? If I'm concerned about injury, I need to watch my step. If I'm watching my step, I should be able to see any snakes in my path. Hmm... that's interesting. So in my Backpack of Fear, I'm taking a small bottle of "watch your step". Two concerns addressed with one simple item.  My load was just lightened.

As we walk through life, we all encounter our inherent "Fear of Knowledge" which can stop us dead in our tracks. We fear something because we "know" what will happen as a result – i.e. "Touching a hot stove will burn your hand". Generally I would agree, yet magically, scientists and adventurers have discovered that you can quickly dip your bare hand *(under the right parameters/prep/circumstances - *Don't try this at home, kids*)* into molten lead without injury. Molten lead is much hotter than a kitchen stove. Remember that experience can provide great insight, but it can also create needless barriers for us to overcome. When you automatically "know" what will happen, you've already stopped your search for answers or new opportunities.  For example, until recently, we "knew" that Pluto was a planet...now we aren't sure. The truth is, we never *"knew"* Pluto was a planet... we *"believed"* Pluto was a planet. **Big distinction.** No one had ever been there. Who was the first person to stick their hand into molten lead fully "knowing" that a kitchen stove can cause more pain than a person can bear?

When we boil it down into its most basic premise...Fear is simply a tool. It can be used by others to detour you from an endeavor. It can be used by others to control you. It can be used by politicians to validate their points. But it can also be used to inspire. What? Inspire? Innovate? *I would be highly inspired to break my running speed record if I were ever chased by a bear or pack of wolves.* When we begin to address the concerns that make up the fear, we nibble away at the weights in our backpacks.

I realize that my example is an oversimplification for most. But when you think about your "daily life fears, relationship fears, or career fears" in a more positive light *(cue happy music),* a world of solutions and opportunities can present themselves. Sometimes the simple search for an alternate opportunity can help you achieve goals you never imagined were possible...i.e. a bare hand in molten lead...

Instead of saying, "I fear losing my job", let's begin to ask, "What is it about losing your job that scares you?" The loss of income or stability? Your Retirement Account? Your children's education? Your pride? When you are able to look at the foundation of concerns that built the fear, you can begin to patch the cracks or solidify the base. *When you work toward the positive, the negative begins to diminish....*

I wouldn't have you believe that life will always be great. *I mean...let's face it...Sesame Street has had a grouch for decades.* But I will promise that if you can look into one or two items in your life that invoke "Fear", search for the root cause of concerns rather than the lead weight of fear, your pack *will* get lighter. A lighter pack gives you more opportunities for adventure on the trail. If nothing else, it might just give you a smile.

Oh...there is one more fear that we didn't address... What about the Fear of Success? Hmmm....now that's an interesting point. I've met many people who are deathly afraid of succeeding. Are you one of them? I'll be looking for you on the trail...

# Part 1:

## Who Made these "Stupid Rules"?

---

### *Introduction:*

In my life, I've often found myself asking "Who made this stupid rule?" As we get older, we find that some "Seemingly Stupid Rules" from our childhood are in fact useful. Rules such as: *Brush your teeth before bed*, or *Don't watch scary movies before bed*, *Put Money into Savings*, & *Respect your Elders* present valuable lessons for children which can help provide a foundation throughout life. However, for some reason, once we enter the business career world, or adulthood in general, we continue to see more and more rules with less apparent value. (i.e. *That will never work*, *You can't do it that way*, *The Company doesn't value that task...* ) Furthermore, as we age, the reluctant acceptance of these rules becomes

1

easier and easier to justify. "That's just the way it is and we'll just have to deal with it."

If you have ever found yourself asking "Who made this stupid rule?", this book is for you. In the following chapters, I will list some of my favorite "Stupid Rules", but notice a trend in the 3 listed above...They can all generate static rebuttals without the true benefit of "Why". In this book, you will see examples of ways of how I've worked to remove objections, tried to look beyond the mundane and tried to inspire the people around me to achieve their goals.

This book is filled with personal stories from my career to date, personal goals, and examples to provide a little insight into my way of thought. Some of you will roll your eyes, some of you will laugh, some of you might seethe with frustration. But ultimately, I hope that through the examples, you see a glimmer of someone you know, understand them a little better, open your mind to the possibilities around you, and take a few minutes from your day to try inspire those around you.

Since this book is about Goals, Obstacles, and Barriers, please allow me to list this book's goals upfront...

> *1.) Let's remove the unnecessary obstacles and barriers – the spoken or unspoken "Stupid Rules" that hold us back from achieving or even setting our goals.*
>
> *2.) Let's ask "Why Not?"*
>
> *3.) Let's think differently about goals.*
>
> *4.) Let's set the stage for advancement by opening our eyes to the possibilities around us.*

*5.) Let's review the way we measure "Success" and maybe find an interesting thought or two along the way to foster a new idea.*

*6.) Make it a fun and enjoyable book. Generate a few laughs and hopefully provide food for thought.*

I have found that most people I encounter in personal or business life, whether I am presenting an idea for the first time or simply meeting them as a client or customer, seem to view things similarly when an idea is new, viewed as different from the norm, or simply outside of their comfort zone. The obstacles of the "Stupid Rules" we've all lived and operated by seem to impede our progress, hold us back or otherwise dim our outlook on the potential or opportunity. This narrow view of possibilities lends itself to the "I told you so…" phrase we've all heard millions of times in our lives. However, if you are able to view the problem, idea, opportunity, or endeavor with a slightly different mindset, the potential seems to increase, the risk seems to decrease, and the success rates can soar.

We will tackle many of these "Stupid Rules" or other obstacles with specific examples in this book, but first allow me to present an illustration to clarify and set the stage for examples to follow. I have found that most people view a goal, idea, concept, or opportunity in this light…

"Normal" Way

**Goal Achieved**

*To most people, it's all very linear. Form an idea based on The "Normal" Way to accomplish it (or the millions of reasons it 'Won't work') and ultimately succeed or fail.*

*We will discuss how this narrow view accomplishing a task or achieving a goal can leave ancillary opportunities hidden, decrease your overall benefit, and possibly increase your risk of missing the target completely. But look what happens with a mind open to new possibilities and outcomes...*

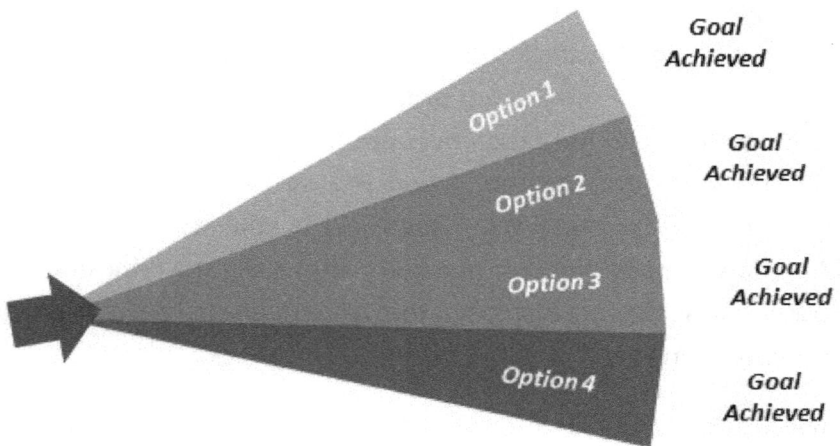

Option 1 — **Goal Achieved**

Option 2 — **Goal Achieved**

Option 3 — **Goal Achieved**

Option 4 — **Goal Achieved**

*Learning to broaden your view by breaking through the "Stupid Rules" that hold us back, dim our enthusiasm, or otherwise detour us from achieving (or even setting goals), can greatly increase our opportunities to succeed in hidden ways we couldn't even previously define.*

In order to remove obstacles or barriers in business and everyday life, we need to ask simple questions such as "What are we trying to accomplish?" and "What stands in our way?" The answers can sometimes be complicated, but I have learned that when I approach situations (Business, Sales, Management, Personal Relationships or Marriage) with these questions, solutions present themselves more readily.

In this book, you will read the word "Should" dozens of times. That's because I feel that we "should" always be looking for a better, faster, easier, more effective way. We "should" strive to uncover the unknown, "should" thirst to be better than we were yesterday, "should" never allow small obstacles to cascade into impassable rifts, "should" allow our dreams to soar and our imaginations to take flight. All of this may sound like a "Pie in the sky" build-me-up opening, but trust me when I tell you... ***Desire drives accomplishment - the desire to work it out, the desire to succeed, the desire to thrive.***

### *Baseline Questions for thought:*

Allow me to pose a few baseline questions. There are no "correct or incorrect" answers to these. They are simply questions I have asked co-workers, customers, and prospective employees over the years. I would like to see your answers or comments as well. At the end of this book, there will be an email address for you to send us feedback. For Question 6, the difference between what we call "Success" and "Happiness" is a matter of interpretation, which only you can answer.

1.) You are approaching an airport ticket counter. You are faced with the snaking rope line to compress dozens of people into a small area. There is no one in line in front of you... Do you:

A.) Skip the rope line completely and walk directly up to the ticket counter?

B.) Walk through the entire rope line and wait to be called at the "Stop Here for next opening" sign?

2.) You are entering a grocery or retail store. There are designated "Enter" and "Exit" doors, but both have automatic door-openers... Do you:

A.) Walk into the closest door, regardless of Enter / Exit signage?

B.) Walk only into the correct "Enter" door?

3.) When calling a business and the call is answered by an automated phone menu... Do you:

A.) Immediately push "0" without listening to all of the options?

B.) Listen to all of the options before making your selection?

4.) When setting goals, do you tend to:

A.) Set a small goal you know is achievable?

B.) Set a large goal you think you have a very small chance of achieving?

5.) Think about your greatest personal or business accomplishment. How was it achieved?

A.) By following the standard prescribed set of guidelines?

B.) By creating your own path?

6.) Would you call yourself Successful? Would you say that you're happy? *(At the end of this book, there will be an email address for you to submit feedback or your personal stories to be included in what I hope will be a follow up series)*

### So…What is a Stupid Rule?

*Merriam-Webster defines a <u>Rule</u> as:*

> **<u>a : a prescribed guide for conduct or action</u>**
>
> **b :** *the laws or regulations prescribed by the founder of a religious order for observance by its members*
>
> **<u>c : an accepted procedure, custom, or habit</u>**
>
> **d** *(1) : a usually written order or direction made by a court regulating court practice or the action of parties (2) : a legal precept or doctrine*
>
> **e :** *a regulation or bylaw governing procedure or controlling conduct*

First, let me say that, in general, rules don't bother me. That may be a strange statement coming from a person who wrote a book including the phrase "Stupid Rules" in the title, but the difference between a good rule and a stupid rule is about interpretation and explanation. Some "Rules" are not written or posted for review. They are simply customs or habits that we continue to perpetually follow without a second thought falling back on the adage "That's the way it's always been done".

Now that we've seen the "Official" definition of a Rule, allow me to pose my definition of a "Stupid Rule" for your consideration.

> **<u>Stupid Rule:</u>** A seemingly self-imposed mandate, condition, custom, or obstacle which serves no clearly-defined purpose other than to dissuade from action, curtail opportunity for advancement, or otherwise provide unnecessary barriers or rigid structure where none is warranted. *In plain English, it is the "Take*

*Away" with no "Give Back", the de-motivating standard that no one can truly explain in a single, one sentence reply to the question of "Why?"*

For the basic litmus test in your personal and business life, the questions to ask are: "Does this Rule help us meet our goals or hinder our efforts?" "Does this Rule motivate our people or cause unnecessary frustration?" "Does this Rule have a reasonable purpose?" More clearly - Where are we trying to go and how does this help us get there?

Here's a good "Stupid Rule" for you…"Adam hasn't been formally trained as an author. He can't possibly write a successful book." *Remember, not all rules are written or posted.* We impose unnecessary rules on people all the time, most without even realizing we are doing it. No, I have not been formally trained as a writer. But if you noticed in the introduction, "Successful Book" was not one of my goals for this book. I have no aspirations of fame or being interviewed by Oprah *(although advertisement is never a bad thing).* The success part of this book for me personally is the chance that a manager, parent, or business owner will glean something useful from my observations and take a different view of how to remove obstacles in their own lives and lives of their employees.


### *Who is Adam Brest?*

From an early age, I *"knew"* I was going to be in sales. I heard all the clichés – "You could sell ketchup to a lady in white gloves" or "Ice to an Eskimo" (*which I'm sure is not politically correct these days*). I embraced these statements and still do today. At heart, I am a Big Picture person – A builder and dreamer. I don't like unnecessary obstacles that obscure the big picture or block our view of the grand scheme. An uncle of mine phrased it best many years ago during one of my visits to extended family over the Christmas holiday. We were talking, as we always did, about my beloved wife, work, our dreams, family history, and where we generally wanted to go in life. As the conversation turned towards the subject of writing this book, he looked me straight in the eyes and simply said, "Bud, you are just one of those people God made without an off-switch." I will never forget that. Many of the thoughts I had about myself were suddenly put into perspective in that moment. The fact of the matter is that I enjoy building, coaching, speaking, and throwing myself into a challenging endeavor. It stirs my desire to succeed, challenges my perception of what is allowable, and sparks the fires of thought within me.

In my career to date, I have sold, what I believe to be, some of the most difficult items to sell to some of the most difficult customers to sell them to. Even as I write this, the thought enters my head that I am continuing this career trend in the pursuit of authoring this book. *Some of you might appreciate the irony of that.* At times, it becomes second nature to take on tasks, which, to the outside world may appear to be whims, but I find are in fact the key to self accomplishment. Not in the grandiose sense, but because you feel you have something to offer.

There is something to be said for embarking on a challenge that some people might view as a whim or as needless. For example, while in high school, we studied the history of Australia and original maritime explorers – Willem Janzsoon and Capt. James Cook. As I researched the topic *(in real encyclopedias in those days)*, I discovered that it appeared the encyclopedia listed both men as discovering Australia. How can this be? Two people can't discover the same thing.

I took it as a challenge and drafted a letter to World Book Encyclopedia. *(Now you're really rolling your eyes...)* I was concise, complimentary of their products, praised them for their years of helping children in the classroom, etc, etc, etc. I politely stated the case for my confusion, listed the Volume #, Edition, Page numbers and other pertinent information to prove my case. The High School office was kind enough to even mail my letter for me. *(Looking back now, I somewhat feel like Andy Dufresne from Steven King's 'Shawshank Redemption' mailing his letters through the warden...)* I never actually thought I would get a reply. I thought they would simply toss out my letter, if it ever actually arrived, or think I was some arrogant would-be attorney, looking to make a name for himself by tarnishing their impeccable reputation.

Much to my surprise, one day the very same month, a letter arrived, addressed to me in the school's PO Box. You cannot even imagine the look on faces of those around me when I opened their reply. *(Although the nervous smile I was wearing as I opened the letter was probably a "Classically-Adam" smirk.)* Looking back, I can only imagine the discussion in the teachers' lounge about this intrepid kid's quest to question the encyclopedia. *Stupid Rule – "Why can't you just let it go and not question it?"*

The letter, with accompanying documentation, was personally signed by their Executive Editor at the time. He graciously informed me I was misguided – but could appreciate the confusion as both statements in the encyclopedia were correct. He informed me that both men discovered different "parts" of Australia *(Main East Coast vs Northeastern peninsula of Australia)*. They simply didn't know at the time that the two discoveries were part of the same continent. He graciously provided copied additional pages from their international version for reference, and politely wished me the best in my future projects.

So why question this? What was the purpose? What can possibly be gained from this endeavor? Let's keep in mind that from "our" point of view, in the present, Australia has long since been discovered. Why dispute a long-established anecdote of history?

The explanation I received came not from the American Version of the encyclopedia that our school purchased...it came from the International Version, of which I had no access to research. Apparently the answer was not readily apparent in the American version. I simply reached out and asked a question few others would. The answer was provided from another point of view - Different author, different edition, different explanation. *The cost to write and mail the letter was nominal. The life lesson for me was invaluable.*

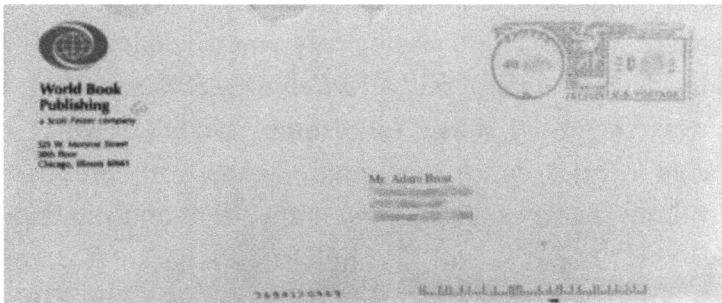

*At least you know I'm not using a Pen Name...*

I guess you could say that I've embraced challenges, large and small, throughout my life. Questioning and learning, trying and sometimes failing, but always searching for an answer – about myself, about the world, and about "Why Not"...

Straight out of college, I moved from my small town in West Texas to Fort Worth and started a small Health and Life Insurance agency as a fresh-faced, naive 20 yr old. Always wanting new challenges, I gradually moved from my Insurance Agency into a corporate career. I've managed sales of commercial paper & packaging goods for a Fortune 200 global company and into commercial recycling & waste services for a mid-sized family

11

company. *Opposite ends of the corporate spectrum.* I've managed truck drivers & sales representatives, built management systems, and created data analysis templates from some of the most structured and close-minded managers. *Trust me when I tell you... they are all as exciting as they sound...sarcasm notwithstanding.* Along the way, I've built a few small businesses, stocked a personal file of product development ideas, created marketing templates for companies, designed corporate branding materials & websites, and led outside sales training and consulting initiatives.

And through it all...time and time again, I find that, as with most things in life, enthusiasm and dedication is infectious. As a 20 year old, brand new insurance agent, I held a 95% closing rate when selling health insurance to individuals - *long before the Affordable Healthcare Act.* It wasn't because I was the most suave, handsome, clever, or witty insurance representative in my area. It was simply because my presentation was different and my clients could feel my enthusiasm and my dedication to them above the "Stupid Rules" that hold others back. *However, I must admit, when it comes to "Stupid Rules", insurance companies win the gold medal...and maybe the silver medal, too.*

At still a young age, when I moved away from my insurance agency and into the world of corporate packaging sales, I set my sights on building a stable and long term account base and found myself managing millions of dollars of corrugated box sales annually. I ultimately moved up the chain into Sales & Logistics management for a small paper mill system handling tens of thousands of annual tons of recycling & waste in my personal account base, leading a team of truck drivers and our regional transportation department, training incoming sales representatives and being the front-person for most of our marketing initiatives and materials. I wouldn't have gone into my history for any other reason than to give you some basic background information about how my thought processes and viewpoints have been formed. The transitions and challenges I've seen from being a small business owner just starting out on my own, into large publicly traded global company in corporate sales, managing for a mid-sized fast-moving private company, and surviving strings of mergers and acquisitions, numerous company name changes and rebranding initiatives all provide the backgrounds I draw upon daily. These experiences formed who I am and how I view opportunities in the future.

I am constantly on the search for a better way to do things, gleaning what I can from other business owners, managers, employees, friends, family, and anyone who will sit long enough to talk with me.  It isn't about being the smartest person in the room - sometimes, it's just about seeing the big picture, being able to lead the room in the direction you want them to go, and always trying to ask the right questions along the way.

With each step, I have embraced who I am, *for what you might determine is for better or worse*, and have embarked on the challenging and personally fulfilling goal of helping managers, business owners, companies, and entrepreneurs align and achieve their goals.  Helping them bring down the unnecessary barriers to success, remove the "Stupid Rules" in our daily lives that can so easily hold us back, and help highlight a roadmap for stability and growth.  Helping them define their targets, opening their minds to the possibilities before them, helping them build marketing programs to seize opportunities, and ultimately creating a few smiles and laughs along the way.

### Some of my Top "Stupid Rules":

1.) Without a college degree, you are not "qualified" for this position.

> *I wouldn't presume to suggest that someone who didn't attend law school could represent you in court or that you would want a medical opinion from someone without training, but, in the general business world, we should look more at the person than the degree on the wall. Remember, there are many companies who "Require" a bachelor's degree for a specific job, without any regard to "What" they received their Bachelor's degree in...*

2.) That idea won't work...Others have tried it and failed.

> *Maybe the people who tried that idea chose the wrong investor, bad timing, or poor planning. I would rather try and fail then to have never tried. I have had ideas in the past that I didn't act upon and I just have to force a smile when I see them succeeding on TV, in stores, or online. I'm sure we've all had these types of experiences. Let's begin to break down the "it won't work barrier" and foster these ideas. The world is full of nay-sayers and devil's advocates who are quick to quash an idea without providing any insight about "Why it won't work".*

3.) Your Salary is based on 40 hrs per week, or 45, or 50, or more...

> *There are some positions that are based on a clock (phone answering, bank teller, customer service), but we should be striving towards a goal and task-oriented work environment rather than a time-oriented work*

14

*environment whenever possible. Someone once said "If you want a job done fast – pay by the job, if you want a job done right – pay by the hour". There is a balance here...Let's find it.*

4.) Salespeople don't make good Managers.

*What makes a "Good" Manager? Some people thrive on tackling challenges of any kind. Some people can see the big picture and others are better at focusing on the task at hand. Some people are fluid communicators and some are natural leaders. Who arbitrarily set the universal standard of a "Good" manager? For that matter, who set the standard for a "Good" employee? What is the task and how do we best accomplish it?*

5.) Commissions/Incomes are capped at $XX/Career Path Progression is limited.

*I heard something years ago which has stuck with me. You can substitute various words into this phrase and still not change the overall concept. "People only value / respect / trust the company as much as they <u>feel</u> the company values / respects / trusts them." (More on this statement later in the book.) This simple statement resonated with me years ago and it seems to work in family, parenting, sales, and business applications. Why would you de-motivate your people by placing limits on income, advancement, or ideas? If your company's goal is to grow profitably, let's design programs that translate value to employees and provide opportunities for personal* *growth. For motivated people, nothing turns a "Career" into merely a "Job" faster than the brick wall of income/advancement restrictions.*

6.) Your overall credit score is not influenced by your income & some debt is a good thing.

> *Loans are based on your income and payment history. Your credit score is a large factor of loan approval. Why is your income not factored into your overall credit score? Credit agencies make assumptions of your income level based on your purchase history. If you don't fit into the "normal" mode, you could be unjustly penalized. Why should you pay interest dollars for things you can afford simply to have some debt to show payment history? Who made these stupid rules? And, if we are all judged the same way, why can't these rules/calculations be posted for critique/adjustment?*

If you ever meet me on the street, feel free to ask me about any of these rules. I can't guarantee it will be a short conversation, but I like hearing other's opinions regarding the rules in their lives. Every time I encounter these rules (or others like them), I am compelled to ask "Why or Why Not?"

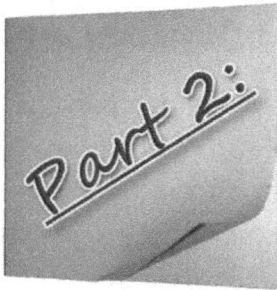

# What?
# No Psychological
# Analysis?

It wouldn't be much of a "Do it differently" book if we contacted the standard psychological community for a tired old detailed analysis on conventional wisdom... Granted, it would be a great opportunity to generate a very nice section of charts and graphs for you to illustrate the point and look very official, but let's keep confusion aside and focus on the heart of the matter.

As I see it, most people are classified with broad-brush labels. There are rule followers and rule questioners. There are detail-oriented people and big picture people. There are talkative people and quiet people. Some are initiators and some are followers. *(More on building a team of allies in a later chapter)* Remember, there is nothing particularly negative or inherently hindering about any personality type. The trick is to know who you are at heart and how you best operate, then expand your horizons from that point. If you're a manager, learn your people and manage to their strengths. As a wise man once said, "Remember your audience".

Take the picture below, for example. You are one person...Bob or Mary, Billy or Sue, Adam or Suzi, but you can also be a Parent, Employee, and someone's child at the same time. Are you exactly the same person, in every situation? Do you speak to your children the same way you speak to your co-workers, supervisor, or team members? Do you handle personal issues the same way you handle issues at work? The general idea is that your overall personality might be set or easily classifiable by psychological standards, but your thought processes and specific traits which surface in different situations can vary and change over time. Hence the importance for being open to possibilities you might not have considered before.

*In the following illustration, You are the Employee or Manager, but you are also a parent, coworker, and someone's child/subordinate. Three vastly different arenas of thoughts and actions, but you are still the same person inside. Food for thought...*

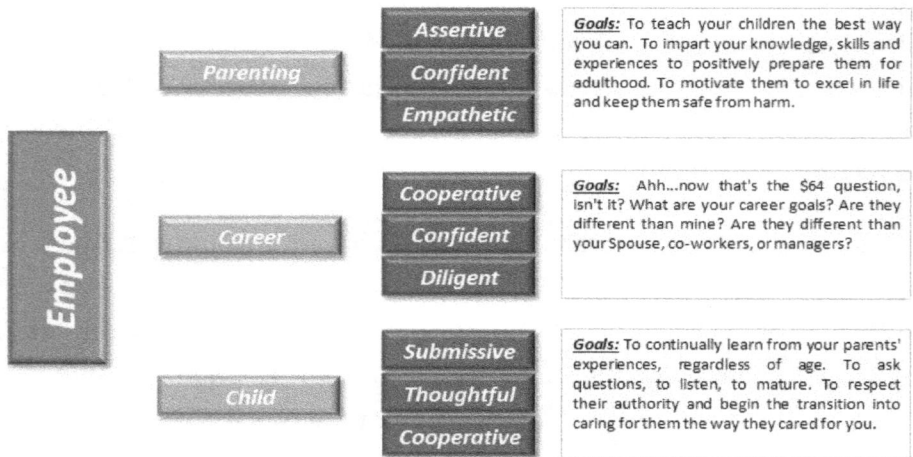

**Employee**

**Parenting**
- Assertive
- Confident
- Empathetic

**Goals:** To teach your children the best way you can. To impart your knowledge, skills and experiences to positively prepare them for adulthood. To motivate them to excel in life and keep them safe from harm.

**Career**
- Cooperative
- Confident
- Diligent

**Goals:** Ahh...now that's the $64 question, isn't it? What are your career goals? Are they different than mine? Are they different than your Spouse, co-workers, or managers?

**Child**
- Submissive
- Thoughtful
- Cooperative

**Goals:** To continually learn from your parents' experiences, regardless of age. To ask questions, to listen, to mature. To respect their authority and begin the transition into caring for them the way they cared for you.

You might be more assertive with your children (or employees as a manager), because you are driving them toward a specific overall goal or teaching them a lesson. You might be more cooperative, quiet or submissive at work because you may not be in a position of ultimate authority and you want to advance your career, learn additional skills yourself, or simply not rock-the-boat. These subtle differences surface naturally every day without a single thought. Even as someone's child, there is an evolution as you age in how you respond to your elders. We are filled with hard and rigid, time-honored, unchanging broad-brush personality traits, but yet every day, different minor traits can bubble to the surface.

If we are willing to accept that as a single person, we can allow different traits, thought processes, and responses within us to surface depending on the situation, then we should be able to learn to view and appreciate alternate options and possibilities. If we can start to change the old rigid ways we view goals, success, failures & rules and begin to question just a little more, perhaps some of the resistance to alternate ideas and the firm grasp on some of the "Stupid Rules" we encounter in our lives might just fade away.

What type of person are you? More importantly, what type of person do you aspire to be? What type of people are your children, spouse, employees, coworkers, or managers? When faced with a task and your mind traces the steps along the way and the order you must complete them, do you skim over the seemingly small details and focus more on the overall task? Do you take one step at a time following a set of instructions? Do you color outside the lines a little now and then? Knowing this about yourself, your family, and your co-workers is an amazingly beneficial piece of knowledge that we will address later in the book.

## The Dreaded and Feared Personality Survey:

I've taken several Personality Profile Surveys in my life and, much to my beloved wife's chagrin, I seem to test the same way each and every time. *(As I think about that...maybe I shouldn't admit it...years and years...and the same result?)* I'd like to think I've certainly learned a lot over the years and I'd like to think I've grown and matured over the years. *(After all, I know which is the soup spoon and which is the salad plate...)*

I'd like to think that I've become a little wiser from my failures and a little more confident from my minor successes. Perhaps, it is simply the way I test or simply the type of person I aspire to be. I've only taken the personality tests with one goal in mind... to advance my career. The traits in the back of my mind, consciously or not, are Big Picture, Forward Thinker, Fast Mover, Positive, Optimistic, and Upbeat. Had I been taking the tests under different circumstances, would I have responded differently? I guess we will never know. From all accounts, the tests pegged me solidly from the outside perspective based on the way I present myself in daily life to those close to me.

It seems that each test has its own branded moniker for my personality type. The one that intrigued me the most was "Daredevil." Suffice it to say, I was labeled as lacking in detail, a go-getter, the consummate sales person, high energy, strong willed, and savvy. *(I presume taking on the challenge of authoring this book is the best testament to the accuracy of the tests themselves.)* But where one manager might read "hard to handle" or "difficult/stubborn" others might read it as "game changer" or "natural leader". It's all in the interpretation of the reviewer and the goals they are trying to achieve. The test itself is not a barrier, in fact, I think they provide great insight into an individual; however, we must be careful how we label people and relate it to the task at hand. As you read this book, you will undoubtedly develop your own thoughts about me, my personality, my views and thought processes.

Allow me to give you an example of why we should be careful about how we slate or define people *(and their ability to succeed or thrive in a position)* based on a Personality Survey Result/Personality Type vs. what we perceive about the individual and their goals or motivation. I received the "Daredevil" personality type result as part of the interview process for an open position with a company years ago. We went through two rounds of interviews and as I was speaking with the Owner/MGR about my personality type, a funny thought struck me.

We talked about compensation, goals, futures, the specific industry, our experiences, funny stories, successes and failures, but I had not asked about their benefit package (Medical Insurance Package, 401K Plan, Dental Insurance, etc) before they sent me their offer letter. I joked with them as I reviewed their offer letter saying, "Now you must really trust the personality survey results because I had not inquired about the benefit package during the interview process." *(The simple fact was that I didn't view it as "Lacking in Detail", I simply assumed by the basic size of their company, that it would be a standard insurance, retirement, benefit package that you would get from most companies.)* I made an assumption about them and they could have made an assumption about me, validated by their Personality Test results.

Honestly, at the time, I didn't inquire about the Medical, Vision, or Dental insurance because, because I didn't take any daily medications, I don't wear contacts or glasses, and knew *(from prior experience in Insurance and Finance)* that I could handle the retirement. A major detail that would have been foremost on someone else's mind, was not a big factor for me at the time because it wasn't something I dealt or struggled with on a daily basis. My Top Goal during the interview process was to discuss the overall position, their goals, their experiences, and how they viewed the future – and ultimately decide if I wanted to join their team. For me, if I didn't think that I could succeed with them, that our goals would be aligned, and that I would ultimately be happy on their team, the benefit package would be of little consolation or benefit anyway. What could have been perceived as "glossing over important details" to one person, for me, was simply something that I expected to be included in the offer letter for review.

When I have told the "Daredevil" story to co-workers, family members and team members in the past, they smile and nod their head in agreement. "Oh yes...I can see that" is their basic reply. As I have joked about our different personality types with them, I've asked a simple question - "Regardless of our differing personalities, what problem have we encountered together that we weren't able to solve?" *(Think about that for a moment from your own experiences.)* Although the Personality Test/Survey might have captured my true inner self, or the "self" I aspire to be, how many problems have you truly encountered that you could not find a solution for – either by yourself, with help from a friend, family, co-workers, manager, or stranger? Solutions and possibilities are everywhere, regardless of the personality type. Opportunities are everywhere – you simply have to keep your eyes open and seize them when they pass your way. But try not to form a fast opinion based on a test result of basic assumption about the person... look deeper... question... learn...

A quiet side-note: *The owner of that company later told me that he wanted to speak with the Personality Testing company about my results because their test listed me as "Lacking in Detail", but yet, in our discussions, I appeared very detailed in the way I spoke and the items we discussed.*

## *The Duck Analogy:*

We have all heard the old adage of the duck swimming on a pond. *"Calm on the surface, but their feet are paddling like crazy under water."* As I've gotten older, I've began to realize that there are, in fact, many types of ducks. And furthermore, I have slowly begun to realize and appreciate how the old adages we learned in adolescence, sometimes need to be viewed with a fresh set of eyes. Let's take a brief moment to discuss 3 of my favorite Duck Types. And, much to my chagrin, none of them are copyrighted animations....yet... *(I would gladly accept offers to adapt 'Who Made These Stupid Rules' into a riveting screenplay)*

- *The Calm Duck*
- *The Bobbing Duck*
- *The Upside Down Duck*

*The Calm Duck* – This is the type of duck all leaders, parents, employees and students are taught to aspire to be. This type of duck has been heralded as the quintessential leader. This duck quietly works hard for everything without showing strain or worries. They confidently swim in the direction they want to go regardless of the tide, current, or wind in their face.

*The Bobbing Duck* – This duck shows no strain or worries because, ultimately, the reason they are calm on the surface is that their feet are safely tucked away. They drift where the tide, current or wind may take them. They might paddle to avoid a rock or another duck, but generally speaking they are peaceful, complacent and agreeable ducks.

*The Upside Down Duck* – Let's face it….Then there are just some ducks who try to swim upside down. Their feet paddle furiously in the air, head below the surface, toiling away for everyone to see. Making waves and splashing - working very hard for everything. But alas, they can only drift where the tide, current or wind may take them. They come up for air and to see where they are headed, sometimes causing them to paddle even harder to avoid an obstacle to achieve their goals. But in the end, for all the effort they can muster, they achieve the same result as the Bobbing Duck.

You might be chuckling to yourself right now and assigning "duck types" to people in your life - managers, spouse, coworkers, employees, or family members. *"Well, Bob is definitely a Calm Duck – He is always on top of things. Aunt Mary seems like a Bobbing Duck – She just agrees with anything and doesn't make any waves. And…well… poor old cousin Larry is an Upside Down Duck – he just can't seem to find the ground with a flashlight."*

Would you rather be like Bob or Aunt Mary? That's an interesting question. But one thing everyone agrees on is that no one wants to be the Upside Down Duck. But why not? I happen to love Upside Down Ducks. They inspire me… They have the drive, energy, determination in the face of failure and an unyielding desire to achieve. Sometimes, they just need a swimming lesson or a little nudge in a new direction. If they could simply catch a few moments of traction, they could achieve untold greatness. The trick with Upside Down Ducks is to catch them before they wear themselves out and stop swimming altogether. When confronting an Upside Down Duck, it is important to appreciate and recognize "Why" they appear to be swimming upside down. *(Some from fear, some from previous failures, some simply because they never learned how to swim in the first place.)* We will talk a lot about searching for opportunities in this book. Upside Down Ducks can offer so many opportunities if you simply watch closely. You might not be able to help them learn to swim, but just from the conversations you can have with them, *(when you open your mind to the possibilities)*, you might be able to learn a great deal about fishing strategies or about hidden dangers under the surface of the water.

On the other hand, some Calm Ducks turn into Bobbing Ducks when they achieve their primary goals. Some Calm Ducks recognize their transition into a Bobbing Duck and set new goals when their primary goals are achieved - *they keep striving for more*. Some Bobbing Ducks never set any goals for themselves; they apparently coast through life without ever making a wave...safe and steady. If you blindly follow a Calm Duck, stop and ask yourself a question. Are following them towards *your* goal or toward *their* goal? Hmmm...now that's an interesting point. Are your goals aligned?

Recognizing your basic Duck Type can be important. But the way I see it, it is far less important than recognizing and appreciating what you need in order to become the duck you want to be. In this discussion about types of ducks, I'm quietly wondering if anyone caught the one thing that all ducks have in common. **_All Ducks can Fly_**... Think about that for a moment. Sometimes the Upside Down Ducks have trouble swimming because they are so used to flying.


### _The Financial Planner and the Couple :_

During the editing process of this book, I heard a story that illustrated my duck analogy perfectly.

A CPA/Financial Planner was meeting with new potential clients. They were a married couple, presumably in their mid 50's. They had been married for quite some time and were working on the issues of retirement, market fluctuations, and a legacy for their children, among other items of note. During several meetings, the wife handled most of the discussion with the broker. She was savvy. She was firm in her desires, she stated, with conviction, the goals they wished to attain. They discussed fees, miscellaneous costs, estimated returns, goals, ethics, and the general sense of how the broker would handle their business.

After the meetings, the broker made an interesting comment to a colleague. "I don't know how her husband deals with her in regular life." He continued, "Her husband barely said two words during any of the meetings." To the broker, she seemed as though she led the charge – A Calm Duck – while her husband sat quietly to the side, uninterested in the proceedings – A Bobbing Duck. He assumed this translated into their daily lives as well.

As you might have guessed, I would love to be able to meet these clients and get to know them. I want to hear their story. I have too many questions left unanswered. This happens all too often in life. People make a quick assumption based on one setting/experience/or happenstance and simply move forward believing their assumption to be fact.

Allow me to pose a few simple questions for thought.

1.) What does the Wife do for a living? Perhaps she works/worked in accounting or finance. Perhaps she deals with dollars and cents on a daily basis. Perhaps she has a business degree or teaches math. Perhaps she handles the financial side of their family's business. Perhaps she simply wants to see how the broker handled adversity.

2.) What about the Husband? What does he do for a living? Perhaps he knew that his wife had researched more options in preparations for the meetings and he trusted her judgment in the financial arena. Perhaps he simply didn't feel well, so she took over the discussions in their meetings. Perhaps the couple's goals were aligned and it was simply easier to have one voice conduct the business.

3.) Perhaps, as in most things in life, one of them was simply more interested in the subject matter than the other.

The broker only knew the couple in one setting – his office – and pertaining to one subject matter. His perception was based solely on their brief interactions. His perception might hold true moving forward in future meetings regarding their retirement, but probably doesn't hold true in every aspect of their life. Instant perceptions can be fickle. *(Remember my story about me not inquiring about a company's Benefit Package during an interview process?).*

We can chuckle as we discuss Duck Types and assign them to people in our daily lives. But we must never lose sight of the simple fact that we all transition from type to type throughout our lives and in different situations. You might be a Calm Duck quietly swimming toward your personal life goals, but the outward appearance to coworkers is that of a Bobbing Duck simply coasting through career life. When pitching a new idea, new way of thinking, or a seemingly "outside view", you might appear to be an Upside Down Duck to those you encounter.

As we begin to think differently and question the status quo to find new paths, foster new ideas, generate new viewpoints and learn new methods, we will find that it matters not what type of duck you are in the water. The real magic happens when the flock begins to fly toward an aligned goal – be it migration or to avoid danger – every duck is part of the team.  They all lead at some point and they all follow at some point in the "V" formation. Although the Personality Profile might be a valid assessment for that person, let's try to use the information gleaned not to discount the person's abilities, but to find the best way to help them fly...


## *A Simple "Solution – Perception" Test:*

Let's try a quick non-official personality vs. possibility exercise. *(This can dazzle your friends and frighten your enemies – ok.. not really, but it makes an interesting point about how everyone's mind works a little differently.)*

$$X + Y = Z$$

$$Z = 10$$

Ok, so if we can agree that (Z = 10), what are X & Y? Did you get out a piece of paper and a #2 Pencil?

Below are a few possible and correct solutions.

$$X = Z - Y$$

$$X = 3$$

$$Y = 7$$

What was your solution?

1.) Did you just neglect the fact that $Z = 10$ and simply solve the equation the way you were taught in school leaving you with another equation like $X = Z - Y$?

2.) Did you roll your eyes, scream to yourself, "I can't solve that equation because you didn't give us a value for either X or Y?"

3.) Or, knowing that $Z = 10$, did you simply substitute two numbers that add up to 10 for X & Y?

4.) If you answered #3, were they both positive numbers or did you get clever, trying to foul up my test, and throw in a negative number like $-20 + 30 = 10$?

5.) Do you hate Algebra and skip this altogether to secretly check your Facebook page to see how many Likes your kitten with the ball of yarn video has received? (*I can hear it now...No one told me there would be math in this book...Don't worry, I don't like math either.*)

The point is that, regardless of our personality type, we all view problems differently, based on our experiences and personal history. In this instance, who's to say your answers aren't right and, if you can back them up, who's to say you're wrong? Where Algebra would teach us that there are very few solutions, and everything has a logical answer, the real world rarely gives us a detailed list of variables to contend with to solve a problem. And furthermore, rarely gives us the answer in the back of the book to confirm our answers as we search for a solution.

Your personality, your personal experiences and history, your personal successes and failures make you who you are today. They are an integral part of all of us. We will discuss "Building a Team of Allies" and "Aligning Goals" in later chapters, but I always try to remember (and remind my teams) that regardless of the problem, keeping an open mind to alternate possibilities and solutions can be a great source of strength.

I might be a self-proclaimed "Big Picture" person and a personality test might have said that I'm lacking in detail. Actually, *(please don't tell anyone)* I can be very detail-oriented when needed - business valuation analysis, website design, line-by-line accounting reviews, HTML Code work, and database building – *(you know, all of the things that put a fire in our souls, make our hearts race from excitement - the things that would compel thousands of us to stand in line for days, just per chance, for a small taste)*. But I find that while the detailed portions of these tasks are necessary, achieving the ultimate goal is what truly drives me. It's the process of working ever closer to accomplishing our target, our goal, our success.

The trick I've learned throughout my career is to determine where we are trying to go, to what level the details truly matter, and which details/ obstacles/ detours/ ancillary opportunities can be handled or seized en route. *(In math or statistics terms, how close do we need to be – i.e. standard deviation).* Once we truly understand that concept, then we can remove some of the "Stupid Rules" that, so often, cloud the bigger picture. A lot of people might automatically perceive as viewpoint as nonchalance or indifference, but, regardless of personality, I feel that opening your mind to possibilities and new ways of thinking can easily trump the perceived risk of possibly missing a few details along the way.

*The Round Pen* - A few years ago, on vacation with family, I helped assemble a round corral pen for trapping feral hogs. I was told that they wanted the pen to have a 30' diameter. I thought to myself for a moment, pondering how I might best accomplish this task, then, I asked if they had any spray paint. The puzzled look I received made me smile, because I knew that they had no idea why I wanted the spray paint. I knew I had an opportunity to present a new way of solving a problem.

"Have you never seen this trick?" I asked. As luck would have it, we were able to find a can of red spray paint amongst the rusty farm tools and miscellaneous implements in the toolbox. I drove a stick in the ground to mark the center of our would-be corral, tied a piece of rope around the top of the stick and marked off 15' (the radius of the 30' circle). I simply pulled the rope taut and sprayed a dashed line on the ground as I marked the circumference, hence completing a 30' circle. *(Oh friends, it was a beautiful circle that would bring tears to your eyes… ok, not really. It was just a painted circle on the edge of a hay field.)* For me, this was the easiest way I've learned to draw a quick, easy circle. They had never seen this trick through years of building round pens. I had no idea how they were used to doing it, but I was there to help and simply did it the only way I knew how.

Was I right? Was my way better than theirs? Who knows in the long run, but it got the job done quickly, easily for me, and they were happy with the result. In this instance, the detail of "How" we drew the circle was basically inconsequential in the grand scheme. The goal was to build a 30' round pen and I simply helped us accomplish our goal the best way I could. Someone might have responded with a "Stupid Rule" of "He won't be much help building a round pen." "We've been doing this for years and know the best way to do it." Remember, how we drew the circle didn't matter as long as the pen was the right size.

I have thought about that story often when I train people. But, as I can rarely shuffle people outside to test all of the ways to draw a ridiculous 30' circle in the parking lot, I simply began to adapt it to something useful in my team's work life. I wanted them to open the eyes to possible solutions, let them know that I am open to receiving alternate views, and remove future minor frustrations along the way by proactively searching for a better way to accomplish a task. In other words, helping them realize that achieving the ultimate goal need not always come with an instruction sheet.

*City on a Map:* When training a new employee, I needed to make sure that they knew our region and could locate cities in the DFW Area. I would give them a simple task without any explanation or guidance. "Please take this Post-It note and stick it within the city limits of Carrollton, TX on the map in the conference room." *(In those days, we had one of those nostalgic Rand McNally 80" wall-sized maps, circa 1972.)* Later that day, I would check the map to see if they had completed the task. It was a great opportunity to provide instant positive feedback with a nice pat on the back and paved the way for a great learning experience. "What's so great about sticking a Post-it note on a map?" you might ask. I would simply tell the new person, "Great job on the Carrollton thing." I would smile and would invariably get a smile in return. The puzzled looks I received were great as they tried to hold back the same burning question you might have had "What's so great about sticking a Post-it note on a map?"

*My explanation:* It is important to remember when I asked you to stick the Post-It note on Carrollton, that I gave no guidance on how to orientate the note, the timeframe in which it needed to be completed, detailed instructions on "how" to find it on the map, or even to let me know when the task had been completed. I could have given ridiculously detailed ways to find it, from first finding Fort Worth, then heading east to Dallas via I-30, north on I-35E, and back west on I-635. But I didn't. In my mind, telling you how to find it for this simple task would be like one of the "Stupid

Rules" that need to be questioned from time to time. There are, in fact, dozens of ways to find a city on a map. And that search alone might help them find and locate other cities faster than any route I could have detailed. I would ask "how" they found it, see if the Post-It note was perfectly straight or sideways, and ask them how long it took them to find it. This would give me another opportunity to pat them on the back for positive motivation and gave me a unique insight as to how they solved a simple problem. Knowing how your team, friends, coworkers, supervisors, family, or peers solve minor puzzles can be tremendously beneficial when faced with larger problems to solve or issues to resolve...

Don't get me wrong, when building a car, house, or bridge, there must be order and detail, each piece in its place and in the correct order. But most things in our life do not require such rigidity and what we might find, is that when we question or allow open thoughts to ponder alternate possibilities, we might just find a better way to do something. As a manager, this was a simple learning and development tool for my team members – they could learn a little about me, I could learn a little about them, it provided a positive start, and generated a smile. *We could always refer back to "Finding Carrollton on the map..."*

### *"Typically A-Typical":*

The well-founded personality surveys aside, I like to refer to my personality type and my way of thinking as "Typically A-Typical". *(How's that for utterly non-specific?)* If we really stepped back and looked, I think we all have a little bit of that in us. When performing sales training, I have often been asked for a sales script by incoming reps and new-hires. I *hate* sales scripts...and I'm using the word "hate" on purpose for dramatic effect. The thought is that a successful sales person could make anyone off the street successful as well simply by having them read a script and scribing catchy comeback answers to stock questions. The fact is, every sales call is different, every customer responds differently, and every sales rep is a different person - Just as every parent, child, employee, and manager is different. Typically A-Typical.

For any of my past customers who read this book, this phrase might look familiar. "I grew up climbing on pizza boxes in a warehouse." Don't worry Mr./Mrs. Customer...it _is_ true. I did grow up climbing on pizza boxes, toy boxes, auto part boxes, and medical boxes in our family's corrugated box plant in a small town in west Texas. The point is that my personality lends itself to telling stories or speaking of personal experiences - many of which you will read in this book. I did not grow up on the streets of New York or in the vineyard-rich region of Napa Valley. Your personality is built upon your history, experiences, and mentors just as mine was. I might be able to write a "perfect" sales script to sell widgets, boxes, or insurance, but it would be a great script for me for a single particular customer on that single particular day...your success would be based on how you adjust it to fit your style and the customer. If this is true in sales, then why do we expect everyone to accept and follow rules the same way? (Parenting, Management, or Relationships)

My mentors, for good or bad, have all been people who looked at life a little differently. Very few of them took a "normal" career path – some by choice and some by circumstance. Some saw opportunities and pounced. Some made their own opportunities. But one thing sets them all apart..."Stupid Rules" didn't stop them. "Conventional wisdom" didn't dissuade them, they kept their eyes open for any opportunity and seized the chance to succeed.

Years back, I met with an investor, not much older than myself at the time, about a business startup I had planned on the side. He told me something that I will never forget. I made a passing comment as we sat in his ornate conference room, adorned with a rich wood conference table, leather chairs, large glass wall of windows overlooking a greenbelt of trees and manicured grounds – the type of conference room which exudes a general atmosphere of wealth and confidence. I simply commented at the end of a our meeting, "I had $XXMM liquid, I would purchase "XYZ Inc." (a specific business I knew was coming up for sale soon thereafter). He smiled and simply responded, "Don't ever worry about the money. The money is always there if the idea/business is good." I left our meeting with a profound thought...that some people go through life with their eyes wide open always looking for opportunities. He wasn't worried about what the "Rules People" would say. He was interested in the opportunity itself and his perception about the person making the pitch.

After this meeting and several bank meetings about this business and other businesses for sale in the months thereafter, I perceived a problem in the way that banks/investors reviewed a business and I began to work on a solution for myself. Most Bank Presidents and business lenders are very "Rules Oriented", as you can imagine. They have to be to a certain extent, but some of these issues are created simply from a lack of asking the right questions and looking at the situation from a different point of view. The issue – How can I remove some of the bias from the way different investor groups, banks, CPA's, and business owners value or otherwise view a company? I thought, there has to be a better way to showcase performance – especially when one is purchasing a business as a launching pad for growth or integration. I studied, researched, trialed, tested, revised, adapted, presented and adjusted until I had created a universal template for assessing the potential risk/value of a company based on its industry and performance. Not only could I compare multiple business against each other, but during investor meetings, I could visually, instantly, and accurately input variables for discussion/review to track changes and manage growth. A few months later, my startup Merger Value was born.

During the trial phase, I met with CPA's, Bank Presidents, and business owners. In one meeting, while speaking to the head of SBA lending for a large bank in Texas, the Manager stopped me and simply said: "I have 2 words for you…" *You can imagine where my mind went…and it wasn't a pleasant thought*…she simply finished with: "Bless You." "Do you know how much time and hassle this could save us?" Another bank Vice President told me, "I've been doing this job for 15+ years, and I would have loved to have this tool along the way." They weren't worried that I wasn't a CPA or have an MBA in Accounting/Finance, they were simply happy to have a new way to save them time, a new way to look at a comparison, and a new idea to help their clients. The response was tremendous and it was solely due to a simple thought… "Why not try something new?"

I was told "That will never work – lenders won't accept it", and yet, of the people most restricted by rules, I was able to make a dent in the "Rule Armor". I would call that a Typically A-Typical result. Did I start out to begin a consultant company, business valuation company, or market analysis company? No…I had originally met with a single investor about a simple start up. But it opened my eyes to other possibilities and led me down the path I'm on today. Each door or opportunity seized, opened another path to consider. Each path considered presented another opportunity for personal growth. And such is the path when you open your mind to the possibilities that lay before us all…

## It's as simple as sliced bread...

As we discuss the search for opportunities, it never ceases to make me smile when I ponder this simple question. Why was the electric bread toaster invented roughly 30 years before commercial baking operations actually sold sliced bread? How did it take 30 years to figure this out this simple innovation? Although I wasn't alive at the time, I imagine the board room debates in the smoky conference rooms of the early 1920's baking conglomerates. Those same conglomerates who were blissfully unaware of the impending Great Depression which was to begin mere months later. "People own bread knives and they like slicing their own bread...We think this 'Sliced Bread Issue' will pass. It's just a fad..." Or perhaps, it was the evil Bread Knife conglomerate in secret collusion with the Baking Board Members, trying to keep the manual bread knives as king on the tables of every American household...

I can just imagine a 'Typically A-Typical' lone wolf scientist and inventor, toiling in anonymity in a dimly lit shop with this simple idea of an automatic bread slicer. Meanwhile, local banks, his friends, family, and investors were probably filling his head with the same objections. "People have been slicing their own bread for thousands of years...It will never work."

So what happened? The commercial bread slicer was introduced in 1928 and became so popular, it was adopted by bakeries across the United States by 1930. As it turned out, partially due to the sheer convenience, people ate more bread. It opened the doors for easier marketing and increased sales of jams, jellies, toppings, and bakeries. By 1943, because of unyielding success, with increases in flour costs and wartime conservation initiatives, US Officials imposed a short-lived 3 month 'Ban on Sliced Bread'. Now just imagine being a mother, father, or child in 1930 when you could actually have easy toast every morning without the need to slice your own bread.  It was such a simple cause, but was adopted so quickly and is now so ubiquitous in our lives today.

Sometimes our focus should not be on changing people, but changing the circumstances around us. What are we trying to accomplish and how can we get there? What is standing in our way and why? Why Not Try?

What is your Sliced Bread innovation in life? It may seem like a strange question to pose, but take a moment and think about it.  Don't worry…I'll wait… If we walk through life with our eyes open, looking for ways to improve and grow, you may find that opportunities literally fall into your path.  You don't have to be an inventor, scientist, manager, or CEO.  It isn't about inventing the *"Best thing since sliced bread"* which, in and of itself, was the *"Best thing since packaged bread"*. It is simply about removing objections and clearing the way to achieve your goals. In management, I constantly ask my team members how they feel, what they like, what they don't like, and encourage them to challenge themselves.  You have to understand that everyone's mind works a little differently and what may seem like the best course of action for you, might not be the best way for them to accomplish a task. Remember finding Carrollton on the map?  Ultimately the same result, achieved a different way.

A recent "Sliced Bread" moment for me was after I was promoted to begin managing our trucking fleet along with sales management.  Diving in head first and managing for the first 30 days, it was painfully apparent that we needed to change the old ways we had grown accustomed to in the years prior. The market had changed, customers were more interconnected, and Just-in-Time service was now firmly entrenched. Feeling that the current system was not adequate for the growth, I created a completely new scalable and adjustable dispatch system *(created using a widely available database program, which was already loaded on all of our corporate computers at the time)*. This new system had the capability to store large amounts of historical data for analysis, forecast customer needs, analysis & track our results, and provide ease of use for driver scheduling. Once I had the base system built, I fought to create a new position for our company - Logistics Clerk. I worked with upper Management, Accounting, and Operations to build the job duties for Human Resources. At a time when "Headcount" was a main area of focus, I worked around the objections, stated my case, highlighted the benefits, and was allowed to proceed. This company had never had a Logistics Clerk before, but I was convinced that for stable growth, efficiency tracking, development, and ultimately increased profitability, we needed this position. The "Stupid Rule" of "we cannot possibly justify a new position" melted away in short order.

Within 3 months, we were able to provide data we had never been able to track, provide individual customer profitability models based on fact rather than conjecture, our efficiency and productivity improved, downtime was reduced, profit margins were tracked and most importantly, Customer Service was elevated paving the way for long-term stable growth. The 'Stupid Rules' of "We cannot increase headcount", "We don't need this data", "Your time is more valuable elsewhere.." were proved invalid in short order.

What were the overall Itemized Results?

1.) Efficiency improved so quickly that the new low-cost hourly Logistics Clerk position removed a high cost hourly driver and his overtime completely from those particular types of trucks. We were able to transfer him into another type of truck we had never had the available manpower to be able to operate internally before. *Expanded Service, Production, and Capabilities.*

2.) The remaining drivers' schedules & hours were stabilized / standardized increasing morale. *Fewer Objections = More Smiles*

3.) Customers could receive up-to-the-hour details, ETA's, customized reports, and deepened their relationship with our company. *Customer Service = Long-term Success*

4.) We were able to accurately amend/revise customer schedules to maximize our profitability and routing. *Lower Cost / More Profit*

5.) We ran ahead of schedule being able to forecast customer needs instead of simply reacting when customers called. *Seamless Service = Reduced Complaints*

This small change will become engrained in the company and customer's relationship fabric. It will become as common for the customer as pre-sliced bread for their toast is on their breakfast table.

Why do I like varying personality types? Why should we look for different viewpoints? Because, as a group, we've all been trained to think linearly in most areas and situations. Broadening our scope by including these alternate personality traits and views allows us to think freely and ask the right questions... leads to innovations... leads to new solutions... leads to growth and new opportunities.

### *The Notorious Pig #3:*

We have probably all heard the story of the best high school prank hoax ever perpetrated. For those of you who have not heard the story, allow me to present it now for your giggling pleasure. *Trust me...this is leading to a wonderful point that you don't want to miss.*

So the legend goes, several high school seniors rounded up 3 pigs from a local pig farmer. They proceeded to smear the pigs with oil and number the pigs - #1, #2, and #4. The pigs were let loose on the unsuspecting school house to roam the halls and cause mass distraction and disturbance to the school day. *(Growing up, as I did, in West Texas, I can certainly appreciate how easily this prank could have been perpetrated and how ridiculously humorous the story still is to me, even now.)*

Once the pigs had been unleashed to do their evil bidding in the hallways of academia, children were quickly ushered out, the local sheriffs were called, and the school day was abruptly ended as the authorities began the task of wrangling the oiled pigs. It was quickly apparent to all concerned that the pigs were numbered. And, with much hassle and grief, Pigs #1, #2, and #4 were quickly captured. But as the day continued, minutes turning into hours, the coffee flowing, sweat on the brows of the local authorities, the tempers of the school officials raging, the search continued for Pig #3. I can only imagine the dim sight of flickering fluorescent lights in the empty hallways of the closed school. Greasy trotter tracks on the floors and scattered homework assignments blowing like tumbleweeds in the corridors. The faint sounds of police radios and the frustration on the voices of those workers embroiled in the tumultuous search for the elusive Pig #3... Alas, Pig #3 was never found...

I love this story for so many reasons. Hours spent in the search for Pig #3 because no one ever bothered to ask the simplest question of all - "Why are these pigs numbered?" It is a wonderful illustration of how we are consistently hindered by the "learned" notions of linear thought. I can hear it now..."There is a Pig #4, there HAS to be a Pig #3..." *(I understand and appreciate that for the safety of the children in this story and to remove potential litigation, the authorities have to make absolutely sure that there isn't another pig waiting to cause more trouble locked away in a closet somewhere...)*

I would like to pose this question for thought. Are there any Pig #3's in your life? Those simple items we fixate upon which hold us back, delay

41

our progress, and turn us into Upside Down Ducks simply because we aren't asking the right questions?

I recently had conversation with a friend looking into retirement income options. He is on the back end of his corporate career and wants to earn extra money during retirement doing something he truly enjoys. (*Turn a hobby into income...I love this train of thought*.) I have had numerous conversations with him over the years regarding this topic. His individual interests and dreams have changed slightly over the years, but the overall goal is the same. I love trying to inspire him and help him foster his dreams, but Pig #3 always derails his ideas before they can fully take root. Taking root is the operative phrase here, because his primary hobby interests are horticulture and gardening. Although he has the drive, knowledge, aspirations and vision, the idea of designing a greenhouse and the cost of building one isn't just Pig #3....it's seemingly a entire herd of Pig #3's. It is a giant obstacle standing in his way.

When we focus on "Why this won't work" or "Why I can't do it", we've already lost the opportunity to succeed in our minds. Without the chance for success, why begin an endeavor? *Pig #3 just gained 50 more pounds...* The last time we spoke, I changed the discussion from the overall grand final plan and focused more on the ancillary hidden opportunities. Instead of focusing on the obstacles in our way, step back for a moment and focus on the positives you already have.

"But how do we accomplish this?" "Isn't that simply a half-measure and won't you end up just fooling yourself?" you might ask. I gave him the following example. I've given this example numerous times and I love seeing the looks on people's faces as they quietly begin to think differently about their obstacles and how to resolve them.

## *The Log Across the Road:*

Imagine you are on the Oregon Wagon Trail, traversing the wild old west, making your way to the Pacific Coast. The trail is marked, you have a map, and, although you've never made this trip alone before, you pack your provisions and bravely head onward west. At the halfway point, you encounter a large tree which has fallen across the trail. It had been a majestic old tree in its prime – it grew thick and sturdy, rising over decades in its search for sunlight. But now fallen, it is no longer part of the majestic scenery. It is a giant obstacle on the way to your goal.

You stop the wagon and begin to survey the situation - The first step. The forest is thick on either side and the log is interlaced between other trees removing the opportunity to use your horse to swing the tree aside. As it sits, the trail is impassable. You approach the tree on foot to get a closer view and estimate the tree weighs 500 pounds. Regardless of bravado, you realize that you cannot move a 500 lb tree by hand. What do you do? *(Ponder your options for a minute...I can wait...)*

Some immediate options could be:

1.) You could throw up your hands and give up.
2.) You could turn back east and search for help.
3.) You could turn back east and tell others the trail is impassable to detour others from their attempt.
4.) You could set up camp and wait for help.
5.) You could leave your wagon behind, pack all you can carry and move forward on foot.

But let's view this problem a little differently. What seems like a giant obstacle at first glance might not be as impassable as you think. Perhaps you can't move a 500 lb tree by hand and you can't get your horse into position to drag it aside. *It's as if Pig #3 put the tree directly in your path to frustrate you.*

Do you have an axe or a saw? Can you move a 250 lb tree? One simple cut can make all the difference in the world on your quest to achieve your goal. One possible solution, and there are too many to list here, would be to saw or chop the tree in half. Then, you would only need to move 250 lbs at a time or simply move half of the tree in order to allow your wagon to pass.

You might be rolling your eyes right now, but I assure you, I've seen this exact example too many times. We tend to focus on the giant problem instead of the simple solutions. Finding a solution to move one giant tree is difficult. Finding a solution to move a piece of the tree is easy. *Take a breath, think a little differently, and nibble away at the obstacle.* Ask the right questions... "What Can I Do?" Rather than "Why I Can't Do It".

Now, let's apply this to the issue of the Pig #3. Were we asking the right questions? For my friend who wants retirement income, sometimes it is beneficial to step back from the giant issues of Agribusiness and a large investment in a commercial greenhouse. So in our discussion, I laid out a simple plan for thought.

Why not start with seedlings, in biodegradable paper seed pots, inside your barn, garage, or spare bedroom? *(Turning Pig #3 into a cute little piglet which is easy to handle.)* The specific example I offered was planting/selling geraniums for Mothers' Day. This small positive step in the right direction was all he needed to start the ideas flowing *(The Upside Down Duck gaining traction)*. He began to smile, spoke a mile a minute and over a pot of coffee, we began discussing how a large greenhouse wasn't necessary needed to start him on his way toward his goal. Perhaps, just maybe, we could design a small greenhouse with the revenue from the geranium sales that he could easily add onto as his retirement approached. If you build the greenhouse with this new thought in mind, he could easily add 8' more greenhouse a year simply using the revenue from the prior year's sales – hence, exponentially adding additional revenues year over year. Hmmmmm... we finally asked why the Pigs were numbered rather than fixating on Pig #3. The results can be spectacular.

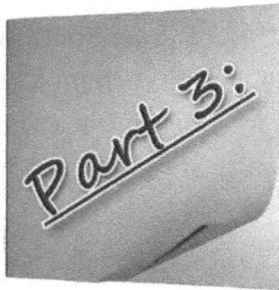

# Motivation & Personability

Personability? Yes, I realize that Personability is not widely recognized as a *real* standard word. But it _should_ be. Perhaps there is an editor for a dictionary publisher reading this book and we can all band together, hand in hand, singing campfire songs and fight to have it added to the English language as my final homage to civilization. Or perhaps, I'm off-target on my soap box and we should just move on. At any rate, please indulge me a minute to explain. My definition of Personability would be:

> *Personability*: The inherent desire to relate to people you know on a deeper level than that of a mere casual connection. A human trait, regardless of career path, age or walk of life, which instinctually draws in passersby with an almost magnetic pull, charismatic charm, and the subliminal knowledge that he/she truly cares for others' well-being.

I strive for this trait – *made up word or not.* I work on it daily and I try to nurture this trait in those around me. *Oh, by the way, here's another "Stupid Rule" for you... auto-correct doesn't like my new word "personability". Red squiggle underlines and auto-corrects are trying their hardest not to let my new word ever see the light of day. But, undaunted, I push onward – red squiggle lines and all...*

Many years ago, I had an interview for an open position with a company who had been a friendly business competitor. I had competed with them for years and they had competed with me. Although I had taken accounts from them along the way, I was quick to tell them in our discussion that they were one of the hardest competitors to sell against. Not because of their price or even their sales representatives. It was simply due to the way they serviced their customers. I arrived early for our appointment, as I always do for meetings, and started a conversation with their receptionist. I greeted her with a smile and polite conversation as I waited for the owner and his team to lead me into the conference room for our meeting.

My conversation with the receptionist could have been branded as "small talk" to the casual observer, but I was quietly able to learn subtle things about the people I might be working with, should our discussions go well and should I had wished to pursue the opportunity. I had just finished asking her a question as the management team walked into the lobby. I stood and greeted them with a handshake and "Good Morning", but before we walked back towards the conference room, I paused, looked at her behind the reception desk and prompted her to finish her reply. I was genuinely interested in what she had to say.

I didn't think much about the encounter at the time. It was simply the way I am - chatting, smiling, and trying to engage those around me. My discussion went very well with the owner and his team that day and when they presented me their offer to join them, one manager quietly remarked, "I knew I wanted you on our team when I saw how you interacted with our receptionist - waiting for her reply, not simply forgetting about her when we walked into the lobby."

I hope I never forget this lesson. The simple act of "Personability" by engaging their receptionist, providing her a smile and perhaps a giggle to brighten her day, hopefully made an impression on her. As it turns out, it made quite an impression on someone else who witnessed it. How many people in your daily life could you provide a smile to brighten their day? Who around you will notice? You might be surprised what you learn about yourself during the journey.

### *Respect and Caring can equal Loyalty and Trust:*

I heard something years ago that has stuck with me. I truly wish I could remember where I heard it, who said it, and how they learned it so that I could give them full credit. *I might have even coined it myself and that's why I can't remember where heard it – when you speak for a living, you're bound to coin a phrase or two along the way, I suppose.* I have used this as my personal motto for years. Every time I meet with a new employee, perform sales training, counsel a co-worker through an issue, or meet a couple with relationship trouble.

It is so deeply magical that even the words are completely interchangeable and it still holds true – *just try that trick with Algebra if you want to see how truly magical it is...*

Regardless of the original source, allow me to present:

> An Employee only ***Values/ Trusts/ Respects*** the Company as much as they ***FEEL*** the Company ***Values/ Trusts/ Respects*** them.

Add Spouse to the equation for a personal life application or substitute Manager for Employee for the reverse angle up the chain of command. Remember this…you will hear it again, I guarantee it. I have held this thought close to me for years now. I remember it every time someone uses the word "Feel". The point is that we all *Feel* our way through life. For better or worse, most conclusions we draw about managers, co-workers, family and friends is simply by how they make us feel. Happy, sad, loved, needed, distrusted, angry, welcomed or valued.

"Feeling" is not a taboo word. Let's not treat it as such. In my career, I cannot tell you how many times I've heard the following phrases from managers, friends confiding in me about their company, or from various management books. *(I truly wish I could tell you that I had only heard them once or never at all.)* "The company has a right to make money off their employees' work." "Those are not *Your* accounts, they are the company's." "You're not the only one who works long hours…" etc etc etc.

Even as I write this, I am sure that you've heard, said, thought the same things over the years. And, although they may be true, I've never found it fruitful to remind my teams or co-workers about these belittling thoughts, much less ever be caught saying them myself. I desired to hear something different from my managers over the years and I made a promise to myself that I would never fall into the same type of management trap where all "Personability" is lost. I chose to take a different path to motivate my team, trying to align our goals, and creating a base of allies for stability and long-term growth.

Perhaps I'm just Typically A-Typical, but for motivated people, one of the worst things I _felt_ I could do as a manager was to jeopardize their motivation by allowing them to change their perception of what they believed was their "Career" into merely a "Job". The motivation for a job is vastly different than that of a career.  People buy into a career with long-term growth – people only buy into a job until a better job comes around.

When I took over as the manager of transportation along with being the Texas Sales Manger in a former life, one of the first things I did was to try to calm the waters after an abrupt transition from the former manager.  I met independently with the drivers, many of whom I had known for several years as a co-worker, but took it upon myself to introduce myself to them and my style as if I was completely new to the organization – simply because they would see me in a different role.  We discussed their goals, their likes, dislikes, we talked, joked and laughed. I tried to put them at ease about where we were headed and that we would get there together _(More on aligning goals later in the book)_.  They knew changes would be coming, as it is with every manager transition, but the calm hand is steadier on the wheel and I knew that what they needed was a calm hand and a positive outlook.

Not losing sight of their _Feelings_, I took a page from my personal life and placed Post-It Notes of encouragement once every week or two on their Daily Route Sheets.  "Be Safe Today – You're doing a great job." "Keep up the good work." "Glad to have you on our team."  Although it might sound cheesy to the outsider, these were seasoned truck drivers with decades of experience – _the same ones a "Stupid Rule" might label as grizzled and coarse_.  I would venture to bet that they had never had a kind word hand-written on their route sheets before I did it.  I would send encouraging text messages when they made a decision that benefited the

50

company and it began to foster more and more positive decisions that ultimately helped us reach our goals.

Did it matter in the long run? I didn't ask if they saw my notes, I never asked for a "Thank you" from them, I didn't look in the trash can by their lockers to see if they simply crumpled up the notes and tossed them out. It was simply because I genuinely cared about them and wanted to give them a smile to start their day. Quite honestly, although I got a few polite "Thanks" along the way from them, the true power of that simple gesture wasn't realized until one afternoon when I met with one of my drivers. He had forgotten to turn in a service ticket during the course of a busy day and I needed him to turn it in before he left so that we could close out the service. When he opened his field folder, I saw my latest encouraging Post-It Note taped on the inside cover. He smiled, pointed, and said that he kept them all in his binder to remind him that he was part of a team.

Although I tried to inspire my team – sometimes you find that they can inspire you just as much.


### *Make 2 Minutes last for Days:*

As with most things in life, who you are is a part of your being. It isn't easily turned off and on, it carries with you. I brand myself to my friends and family as a cheesy salesman, I prod my beloved wife with light sales training along the way to make her giggle. It's just who I am. I try to brighten a day, create a smile, and leave a positive impression. Don't get me wrong, some people just won't like me, won't understand me, or think that I'm just out to get something from them. I can appreciate that, but it doesn't mean that I won't try to change their perception.

I mentioned "taking a page from my personal life and putting Post-It Notes on the drivers' route sheets earlier. I began doing little "day-brightener" things like that many years before I managed a team, drivers, or ever owned a business. My wife would find a little note on the coffee pot, in the pantry or taped to the bathroom mirror. Just an inspirational "I Love you", "Have a great day", or off-color remark – sweet and salty, "I love seeing your smiling face every morning – just because you haven't quite decided how ridiculous I truly am yet." "How can I brighten your day today?" I send close friends and former co-workers texts in the morning with a simple note to let them know I was thinking about them and hope that they have a great day.

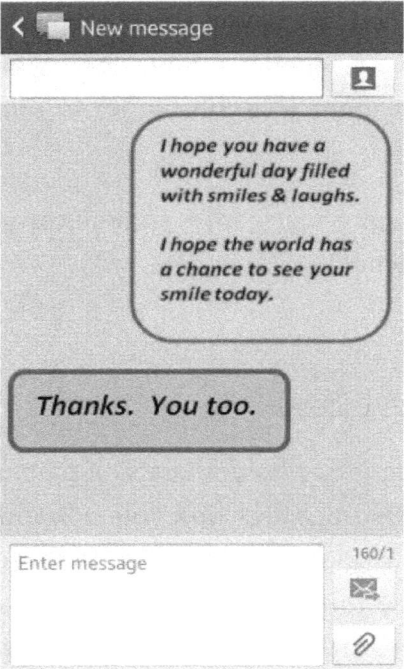

Much to my surprise, they have become so accustomed to them, that when I was traveling for a few days and out of cell phone range, I returned home to numerous texts making sure I was okay. ***Try to inspire those around you...***

On my beloved wife's birthday a few years ago, I awoke before she did. I had her present and a real birthday card that she would receive at dinner that night, but I wanted to give her a little extra brighter to start her day. So I sat at the kitchen table to craft a simple Happy Birthday note. I wrote one note, then another, then another. As I wrote them, an idea for the next note popped into my head and a playful thought occurred to me – I could write several and pick the best one...or...I could just make a birthday scavenger hunt for notes around our home. I scribed 17 notes in all that morning at 5AM at the kitchen table. I placed them all around the house. In her closet, on the bathroom counter, in the refrigerator, the pantry, the coat closet, on the mantle, in her favorite chair, and the last one inside her car.

That morning as she woke and saw the first note, I'm sure her thought was..."Well, that's nice, he didn't even get me a card..." Then she found the second note, then the third. She began to wonder as I didn't say a word about the total number of notes...she simply kept finding them around the house. I would hear her voice from the master bedroom..."Found #12, oooh...#13...How many of these did you write?"

As she left the house for work, she stopped in the driveway and my phone beeped with a text. "Found #17...Thank you. I love you so much." This wasn't about an expensive gift, it wasn't about a grand gesture, or even because it was a difficult thing to do. It simply made her laugh and will be something I hope she will remember for years to come. Her smile and quick steps around the house searching for more notes, the way it made her feel as she started her day, and the way she kept the notes in her drawer to remind her when she every feels down. Just a few minutes can make a big impact.

Now let's adjust the words in my adopted motto: A Spouse/Friend only **_Values / Trusts / Respects_** you as much as they **_FEEL_** that *you* **_Value / Trust / Respect_** them.


### _We are People First & Foremost:_

We've seen how this simple thought can work in your personal life and with your team, whether you're a Manager or not. For Salespeople, the stretch to use this thought for customers is a simple one. I've prided myself in the fact that I've lost very few customers in my career. Regardless of the product, and even in the "spreadsheet bid world" we are in, I try to keep customers for a very long time.

In the "Stupid Rules" of sales, there are many. "That customer is too small to waste time on." "They are too needy." "They aren't the right fit for us." Etc. We've all heard these in our lives – whether you're in sales or not. Allow me to give you an example of one customer that I heard numerous "Stupid Rules" about.

This customer was a national logistics and distribution company. This location, however, was an aging warehouse, boasting minimal activity with a skeleton crew. I stopped by one day while I was meeting with a customer across the street. *(good lesson for anyone in sales to spend 5 extra minutes to at least check out the neighbors...)* I met with the manager, introduced myself and he took me on the grand tour of the vast, yet mostly empty warehouse via golf cart. It was instantly apparent that he was very proud of what they had accomplished in years gone by, speaking of customers they had serviced, types of products they had stored, etc. He was resigned to the fact that they might shut down his warehouse if they ever shipped the remaining customer product he was responsible for to another location. But, unlike a typical salesperson whose mind might have been focused on the business that wasn't there, my focus was on the manager himself. He might transfer to another location in the company, or to another company altogether…he might start his own business in the future…he might be able to refer me to one of his customers. *I cannot stress how important it is to think freely and differently when you encounter these types of situations and to look deeper than the surface. The "Stupid Rules" would have told me to politely hand him my card, exit quickly, mark it off my list as probably never amounting to anything…But I didn't listen.*

The manager and I completed our tour, I had told him what we did and how we might help along the way during our tour – a very soft pitch, and we chatted for a few minutes about past experiences and basic personal histories. Afterwards, we worked together off and on for a year when he had little business projects we could assist with, nothing major, but we kept in touch and tried to make him _feel_ like the important person he was. By our company standards, they were one of the smallest customers I had. But that didn't matter. It was positive sales volume, minimal effort, they were pleasant to work with, and you never know what the future will hold. One day, I popped into his office to say hello when I was in the area. I saw his team searching and itemizing a pallet of customer files. As we had some history, I joked about how miserable that task must be and we laughed about corporate directives. I reminded him that we could help him shred the files when he was done reviewing them *(I assumed that they were his company's old customer files).* It was more of a favor for a friendly customer to ease his life. What happened the next week still shocks me to this day.

I received a call from him several weeks later. "You said you could help me shred these files? I just got a call from corporate legal and they want me to shred them all." *("All?", I thought… "How many is "All?", I secretly wondered)* "I'll be there this afternoon." I replied. When I arrived, he took me into the secure wing of the warehouse where aisles and aisles of pallets were staged, stacked and waiting. 750 Pallets total... My eyes lit up and we worked on the recycling/destruction details that same day. I had the trucking arranged, pricing submitted, the local manager signed, and we got approval from their corporate to proceed within short order. It turned into the single largest net profit from a project for our division that year. From one of the smallest customers I had - to one of the largest project profits of the year virtually overnight. With no bid competition, no long-term time investment in proposals or contracts, and not even a hint of a waiver on whether we were the right company to work with on this project. He trusted me and I was there when no one else was knocking on his door. As the years progressed, I was able to work with 3 additional locations for this logistics company from personal referrals from the single manager I befriended and helped. From our conversations, he felt that I was more than a sales guy, spoke to him differently, and didn't merely drop off a card, never to be heard from again.

Many business owners, other sales managers, and team leaders will hate this story. Trust me, I know how rarely this type of customer gem occurs. However, my focus was not on the volume from that particular customer, it was about building a relationship with the manager for something down the road. We completed the project and eventually, they closed the facility. The manager moved on to manage another larger location for the company, and I continued my relationship with him and his company for years. A few minutes of my time lasted for years...

## _Gems are all around us:_

Everyone has a story of finding a gem in an unexpected place – just like my customer example in the previous section. Maybe it was a customer who started small and grew into a large corporation. Maybe it was chance encounter in a coffee shop meeting someone would become a life-long friend. Maybe it was your meeting your spouse at the friend's party that you didn't want to attend at the time. Maybe it was the ever-elusive classic-car-in-the-old-barn discovery, or the back-alley restaurant with the amazing menu that no one knows about. Think back in your life and place that thought in your mind of the gem you found.

What were you doing at the time? Was it sheer luck or did you do something out of the ordinary to foster it? Did you recognize it at the time or realize it later? I'm not advocating stopping everyone you meet to chat, but it never ceases to amaze me as I speak with people along the way how willing most people are to open up with interesting tidbits when given an opportunity. I have learned that as we walk through life, hidden gems lay all around us, if you are willing to simply take the time to acknowledge them, talk to people about them, share your stories and listen to their stories in return.

Along the way, I've had discussions with customers about their children, their spouses, their goals, their frustrations and successes, and it never ceases to make me smile. In insurance, I needed to be able to move the relationship from initially introducing myself to, within an hour, walking away with their entire medical history, social security numbers, intimate details of their lives and earning their trust. There was no better training ground for me to learn my definition of "Personability" and finding hidden gems than the years I spent building my insurance agency.

Simply by engaging some of my clients over the years with, what I call "above the business" conversations, I have been able to contact them later when I needed assistance with a project or pass along a referral for their own businesses.  One example which still makes me smile was a customer of mine years ago, that I knew loved hunting.  In our normal conversation one day, I told him that I was starting an online outdoor gear company in my spare time on the side as a little personal project. *My point in telling him was not to sell him any products, it was simply because we both shared a passion for the outdoors and both grew up in small Texas towns.*  He laughed and told me that I should talk to his son who had just started a feral hog hunting excursion company.  He passed along his son's number, I made contact and they became one of the premier hunting excursions listed through my site.  We were even able to develop our own special package together.

I knew that my customer loved the outdoors, but this one single comment in passing about a personal goal turned into a gem instantly. His son's company is so busy now, that they are booked years for in advance and even launched their own TV Show.  It wasn't because of my influence or any work we did together, it is merely a simple example of a hidden gem just waiting to be discovered.

What hidden gems await discovery on your team, with your co-workers, with your family & friends? I recently walked into the lobby of a bank, to make a small transaction.  As I approached the table (where they used to keep deposit/withdrawal slips) I was told that they had gone completely paperless and that the teller could assist me.  I was confronted with the dreaded empty rope line *(which is such a personal frustration of mine)* staring sinisterly at me, taunting me, mocking me... It was after the lunch rush and there was not a single customer waiting for the next available teller.  I looked at the teller, standing behind the counter, looked at the dreaded empty rope line in front of me, sidestepped it with a smile and approached the counter. Smirking, I said with a laugh, "I'm not going to walk through the empty rope line...I'm just not that kind of person."

The teller politely asked me what I was doing that afternoon and how my day was going – basic small talk as she worked on my transaction - I replied that I was working on this book. "What's it about?" she asked. I told her the basic premise and explained the reason for my reluctance to walk through the empty rope line. She smiled and chuckled a little.."What's it called? When will it be released?" she continued to question.  To my surprise, she pulled a Post-It Note from her drawer and wrote down the title. "I will have to read it when you finish."  When I left the bank that day, no less than 3 bank employees waved, smiled, and said goodbye. Not in the "Thank goodness he's gone" sense of saying goodbye *(I hope)*, but more of the genuinely happy demeanor sense of goodbye. They could tell that I was in a great mood, cheerful and smiling, and hopefully, it provided a small boost to their day.

A gem waiting to be discovered? Who knows? I have no idea if she will read this book or if they even remembered me 3 seconds after I walked away, but if I have learned anything in my life, it is that you never know what is behind the next door.  She might like the book and pass it along to a friend. A co-worker might ask her what we were talking about and she passed along a copy of the book title. She might be starting a business on the side and might need help building a business plan. The possibilities are endless. The simple fact is that when you view every opportunity or person as a hidden gem, it changes your perspective on how you treat them, interact with them or simply view the encounter (presently and in hindsight). That's the real world application of Personability to me. The inherent desire to relate to people you know on a deeper level than that of a mere casual connection.  Ask a question, listen, and you might be surprised what opportunities present themselves.

### Sometimes the competition isn't crazy:

In business, all of us have probably heard the "Stupid Rules" of: "That pricing is crazy, they can never support that long term," or "If they want to lose money on that proposal, just let them," or my ever-frustrating "They are an unreasonable customer."

I have encountered these phrases more times in my career than I care to count. They have all fallen flat with me because they come across as the rigid, unyielding "Stupid Rule" of "We know best – Do it the way we've always done it." We fall back on the old business adage of "If you don't know who the sucker at the table is, it is probably you." I try to teach the concept that there isn't always a sucker at the table. Sometimes the "gem" for you, wouldn't be the same "gem" for anyone else.

I'm not much into jewelry, but follow me for a moment. My birth stone is a ruby *(Now the full Leo personality picture is coming together for you...)* Let's just say, for example, that someone found a ruby ring at an estate sale or with a metal detector and placed it in an on-line auction. Let's say your wife, mother or daughter was also born in July. One might say that we have a common interest in this ring because it contains our birth stone. Who else has a common interest in the ring? A jewelry dealer looking for resale value, a collector to add to his collection, a passerby just looking for a deal or because it looks valuable?

The ring owner might have had a formal appraisal performed on the ring, but we would all have different value targets or final pricing in our own minds. I might offer $100 for the ring because I'm not a big jewelry fan – even if it is my birthstone. You might be looking to replace a similar ruby ring that had been in your family for generations. Although it isn't the exact ring, you might put a value of $1,000 on the ring, regardless of the formal appraisal. The jewelry dealer might put a value of $300 on it, because he estimates that he would only be able to resell it quickly for around $600, doubling his money. The collector might put a value of $2,500 on the ring, not because of the actual ring's value, but because of the value it would bring to the rest of his overall collection. Who's the sucker? The auction holder might think the collector is a sucker, but does he know the personal situation of the collector? The jewelry dealer might think we are all suckers – me for low-balling and missing an opportunity, you for paying too much to hold it for yourself for sentimental value, or the collector for "vastly" overpaying. In this online auction, we are all anonymous bidders.

The same thing happens in the business world all the time - business goals competing with personal goals and businesses competing with each other. What might be valuable to you, might not be valued the same way to your competition or to your own co-workers.

I had a customer almost a decade ago that worked with the US Post Office and was a subcontractor for a global courier/delivery service. As their business grew, they extended their hours in two shifts to 16 hours per day / 7 days a week. They became frustrated with our lack of weekend service in those particular types of trucks/service capacity. I was not in a position to change our program, extend our hours, or amend our program at the time *(much to my protest)*, and during a meeting with Management, I was told "They are just an unreasonable customer. No one will provide weekend service for them." *(This type of firm, unyielding discourse infuriates me...)* What happened? I explained my current situation to the customer, we discussed every possible option I was allowed, in our narrow view, to present and we were unable to align our goals. They found a vendor who could provide true weekend on-call service and made the transition. I left our relationship on very good terms and they saw my struggle to keep them as a customer. I was rewarded years later with an opportunity regain them as a customer once we had the capability to service their weekend needs.

*Management view – "The customer is unreasonable, no one will provide that service for them." Well...someone else can and just did.*

*Possible Competition view – "We already provide weekend service and we can steal this account with very little discussion about pricing." Slam Dunk.*

*Possible Competition view – "We have another customer who is begging for weekend service. Adding this prospect as a customer provides enough work and profit to bring on that extra driver and keep our other account happy."*

Remember, there are two sides to every coin. When working with business owners or managers, one of the biggest mistakes I have seen companies make is to judge the value or validity of a competitor's proposals / pricing / methods based upon their own internal numbers (internal costs, outlets, methods, etc). We buy this widget at $5 each and sell them for $7 each. They can't possibly sell them for $5. Do you know their end goal? Do you know their motivation? Do you know their financing or supplier goals?

Have you ever had a car dealer show you their anticipated "loss" on a particular car to prove that you are getting the best possible deal? *(Let's assume for a moment that they didn't fabricate the "cost" of the car and that it is a legitimate invoice cost.)* Why would they ever sell a car at a loss, you ask? It could simply be based upon their volume incentives or dealer discounts from the manufacturer. It could be the end of the model year and they "need to make room for new inventory" as the ads always say. It could simply be that the particular sales rep is willing to forego their commission on this particular car *(commission which could have been included in their "Cost" for the vehicle – hence, the "loss" for the dealer)* in order to make his goal for the month and keep his job. It could be that they know their typical clients purchase many of the dozens of extended warranties, offers, protection plans at closing that more than make up for the "loss" on the particular vehicle. Whatever the reason, another dealer might not be willing to make the same deal.  That isn't being crazy...it's business.

Just as I might not place a high value on the ruby ring in my prior example, that same exact ring might hold exceptional value for another person.  We see it in corporate acquisitions all the time.  What we perceive as an exaggerated face value for a business acquisition might simply be another corporation's way of keeping their primary competitors away from a patent right for an additional 10 yrs.  Or, to reduce tax liabilities, or supplement another area of their business product line, or to simply use some of the value of the purchase in name recognition to enhance their overall marketing strategy.

What I try to teach, and one of the focuses of this book, is when you open your mind to possibilities, you can view your competitor's proposals, pricing, products, marketing campaigns, etc in a slightly different light.  I look for potential everywhere. When I am standing in a lobby of a customer, I chat up every sales representative in the lobby to see what they are offering – *even competitors along the way*. I coach sales people when they come to submit a proposal to me. I walk around the manufacturing floors of businesses and look for learning experiences for myself.  I cringe at some TV commercials and think of ways I would have said the same thing differently.  This isn't viewed under the microscope of judgment, it is viewed through the eyes of improvement and potential for myself and my clients down the road. "Why this?" and "Why not that?"

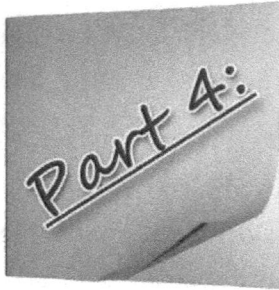

# Part 4

# How do we View Goals?

In business and life, goals are all around us. Finding and defining them can be slightly more difficult. I mean, yes, there are the charity fundraiser goal thermometers with the rising column of funds signifying how their campaign is trending. Some goals are not as visually clear. I was taught throughout school and college to set rigid goals to drive myself, and I did. But as I opened my eyes to alternate possibilities, I have discovered that there is a vast gray area in the ultimate satisfactory completion of most goals. If we simply adjust the way we interpret or view ours and others' goals, then we might open a world of possibilities that we had never contemplated before.

We discussed before about how sometimes the competition isn't crazy. Just as you might not know a competitor's internal finances / circumstances or how they value a particular item or idea, we face unknown goals from others every day. Sometimes we can guess about the goal, sometimes we have to make an informed decision with the limited available information we have, and sometimes we will never truly know the driving force behind one of our competitor's decisions.

### *To an Outsider, some Goals aren't readily apparent:*

Take Warren Buffet and Berkshire Hathaway, for an example of non-apparent *(or non-transparently itemized goals)*. Dozens of books and thousands of newspaper articles have been written about their acquisitions over the years. The simple fact is that, although I would never diminish Mr. Buffet's and his team's accomplishments, they are able to receive special financing, investor paybacks, and put together deals that the regular investor is unable to match. Each deal is different, the value they place on each company is different, it can simply be based on the special terms of each package and the overall goals might not be listed for public scrutiny. It is reported that Mr. Buffet's favorite holding period for stocks is "Forever". If you're in the stock game, what's your holding period? What is "Forever" to you? A "Durable competitive advantage" is supposedly the name of the game for Berkshire Hathaway. It has been defined as an intrinsic value of the brand name, the products, the estimated longevity of their market, and the long-standing history of the business in question.

What gets lost in this equation to most people is the fact that Berkshire Hathaway in itself brings an intrinsic value to these companies. The stated goal might be to "bring value to our shareholders, provide stable long-term returns, etc." But don't fool yourself, the individual companies they own, or hold minority/majority stakes in, are still under the same quarterly pressure to perform as every other publicly-traded company. There are countless goals of each individual company under their corporate umbrella. Dairy Queen has vastly different profit margins, marketing, and performance goals than that of BNSF. Both are owned by Berkshire Hathaway, but both companies are in vastly different industries.

You might not see a connection until you step back and think for a minute. How much of the raw materials for other Berkshire Hathaway companies are transported by BNSF trains? Do they receive special pricing as sister companies? Do they receive priority service? Are they forced to use BNSF when possible to transport their goods? Ah, but wait. They also own Xtra Lease, a trailer leasing option for truck transportation. How many deliveries to individual Dairy Queens are handled in Xtra Lease trailers?

How you put the pieces of the puzzle together, how your competitors put their respective pieces together, and how their individual goals intertwine are not always readily apparent at first. I try to teach the concept of opening your mind to the possibilities around us, look for the opportunities and avoid the "Stupid Rules" of assuming every goal is easy to find or define. How much of Berkshire Hathaway's next acquisition will be a current or future consumer of the products or service from Berkshire Hathaway's other ventures? To an outside investor, the goal might not seem apparent. Luckily, in this case, as a public company, their main holdings and results are public for investor review, which gives us a small glimpse at how their bigger picture could come together.


## *Hidden Sports Goals? Really?*

Now from the opposite end of the spectrum, look at one of my favorite people to follow and listen to... Mark Cuban. He had a vastly different rise to prominence than Warren Buffet. *I doubt you would ever see*

*Warren Buffet on 'Shark Tank' fielding product pitches from someone like me.* But Mark Cuban brings his own intrinsic value to his businesses - his cult of personality, his style & savvy, and, whether you like him or not, his own set of business goals.

Business goals aside, let's take the sports fan angle for just a moment. Many of us are sports fans, be it Football, Basketball, Baseball, Soccer, Golf, Hockey, Lawn Darts or Horseshoes.  For those of you in the Dallas/Fort Worth area especially, I believe we have two of the most influential and, at times, divisive team owners in any respective league – Jerry Jones of the Dallas Cowboys and Mark Cuban of the Dallas Mavericks.

During the process of writing this book, I drafted a letter to both of them asking them both the same questions to get their unique perspectives on the "Stupid Rules" that they encounter in their daily lives or have heard during their journey to achieving their goals.  One might say, "Adam, you are ridiculous. They will never take time to meet with you about your book, much less take time to answer your questions." *(You might be right, but I hope that if the previous chapters of this book about overcoming the "Stupid Rules" that create unnecessary obstacles in our way, you might realize that I would send the letters anyway – remember World Book Encyclopedia?)*  After all, the worst they could say is "No", "I decline to answer," or simply ignore my request altogether.  You will never know unless you try...

I think most people would all agree that these two men are successful.  I think that most people would agree their respective paths to success were both slightly unconventional. But, even with different backgrounds, different paths, different motivations, they both stand today in the rarified air as owners of major professional sports teams in one of the largest markets in the USA.  Both of their teams have stood atop the

Championship mountain of their respective sports, both have savored the taste of success and both have pushed for more. You might have varying opinions of each man and of each team, but I don't think that anyone would dispute the fact that they have shown the tenacity to define their goals, work to achieve their goals, and give themselves and their team the best opportunity to succeed. Sports are mere entertainment for fans but truly livelihood and careers for athletes, owners, agents, and team & venue employees.

From the fan's perspective, we fall in and out of love with individual athletes, cheer for the laundry they wear and play GM & Coach along the way before the draft, during the offseason, or even during each game. "Take him out, put him in, run this play, punt, milk the shot clock" etc. It is important to realize that the coaches, athletes, and owners have a different set of goals than each and every fan. Fans have different goals than each other. That is in part what makes our country great – the freedom to express differing views. We all have different tolerances for risk and place different values on goals. Fan goals are fairly easy for most of us to identify or define. Most of us have the same goals...win. Hold the trophy at the end of the season.

I'm prone to wonder, however, about the owners' goals. I've read about and heard a lot from these two men over the last decade - State of the Team addresses, newspaper & radio interviews. I can't help but wish I could have a few confidential moments with each to listen to how they itemize and balance their business goals vs fan goals. *(Let's face it...as fans, we hope that each owner loves their own team and roots for them more than their fan base does.)* From salary caps, contract lengths, concession & venue costs & revenues, TV revenues, marketing campaigns, licensing values, and their overall "brands" vs. the fan's goal of holding the trophy at the end of the season. Just as you might never know your competition's internal workings, we might never know the true motivation of your local sports team owners.

We might be able to go back historically and calculate how a losing streak can affect season ticket sales or individual game attendance, but how do those factors fit into the owner's overall goals? Does that high-priced aging player still generate huge positive revenues in merchandising sales? What "Stupid League Rules" would they like to be able to remove in their daily lives? What opportunities have they missed, that they deeply wish they could give fans the inside story about? How closely aligned are their goals to that of their fan bases *(whether they can publicly voice it or not)*?

Now that we've taken a brief look at how we view some other people's hidden or stated goals, what about your personal & business goals? Do you have a list of goals? How do you measure them? Are you achieving them? Have you ever helped anyone else achieve theirs? How do you measure your success in achieving a goal? Are your goals flexible or rigid? How many have you forgotten completely or adjusted as you grew older? There are short & long term goals, life goals, career goals, school goals, small goals, big goals, financial goals, relationship goals, etc. Do you have any goals you set simply to challenge yourself? Types of goals which have no bearing on your overall happiness in life, but are simply ideas you crafted in years gone by that stay with you. What are they?

## *My Old Personal Goals:*

Speaking of old goals that stay with us, below are the three goals I created when I was 18-20 years old, full of wonder, single, naïve and energetic. You might laugh, but I still hold 2 of them dear, as ridiculous as they may seem. I'm sure you can imagine all of the "Stupid Rules" regarding these that I heard over the years. "Don't set these types of goals for yourself." "You don't have the right background or enough experience to do that." "You'll learn better when you get older." etc...

1.) Be Earning $100,000 per year by the time I reach 24 yrs old
2.) At some point in my life to own an airplane
3.) Develop/Have a product for sale in Walmart

Why Walmart? Not because of the prestige, but simply because it was the largest retailer in the world. *(If this book is sold through Amazon, then, well...hey, I guess I will mark that goal as achieved – Amazon wasn't around in those days).* I passed 24 yrs old a long time ago and only I and the IRS will know if I achieved Goal #1... but the other two still hold a special place in my heart even after all these years. I liked, and still do, the mystique of being free to fly anywhere at virtually any time in my own plane. I like the idea of seeing a product, born from my mind, take wing and find its way into the lives of others.

Although these goals from my early adulthood might seem far-fetched at first glance, remember that I never specified the size of the plane, never specified in what career path I would achieve my $100,000 per year, and I never specified what type of product for sale. I was, am, and will probably always be, a big picture person and a dreamer at heart. I was never the type of person who taped the magazine page of the newest Corvette on the bathroom mirror to view it every day in the search for inspiration to succeed, as so many sales and business books over the years have preached. But I stowed these goals away, wrote them down, never lost sight of them and have looked for opportunities to arise.

What were/are your goals? Do you share them with anyone else? Did you ever write them down?

My beloved wife and I have been together over 10 years now, and while that certainly does not qualify me as an expert on marriage, I can honestly say that she has never once seriously quashed an idea of mine, never said a serious disparaging word *(other than possibly not allowing me to fly her around in my goal plane until I have years of experience - as most wives would tend to agree)* about any of my goals.

What are the goals driving you? Do any of your old goals still hold a special place in your heart?

### Don't let a "Stupid Rule" change your outlook:

It surprises me how some people miss the fact that personal goals, career goals, and corporate goals intertwine in the fabric of our daily lives. *And, unfortunately, how many of us set a rigid linear goal without the opportunity to expand/adjust/revise along the way to achieve an even greater long-term goal.* Take my "own an airplane" goal for instance. Conventional wisdom would tell you that without a stable high annual income, I would have a difficult time achieving that goal. Not only in the upfront purchase cost, but maintenance, fuel, hangar, licensing, etc. Remember this illustration from earlier in this book - the Linear view of a goal accomplishment? This linear view of plane ownership would lead you to inherently believe that there is only one way to accomplish this goal - *(A fair amount of loose capital).*

"Normal" Way

Goal
Achieved

*(Buy, House, Maintain, Use for personal recreation/business – Hold Asset)*

But nothing is impossible, let's think freely for a moment. Hmm…how could I achieve my stated "Own an airplane" goal? The possibilities are endless when you step back, stop thinking along the linear line of normal, forget the "Stupid Rules" and allow an idea to take root. When consulting for businesses or performing sales training, I teach a different viewpoint to achieving a goal. My "Goal Funnel" looks like this…

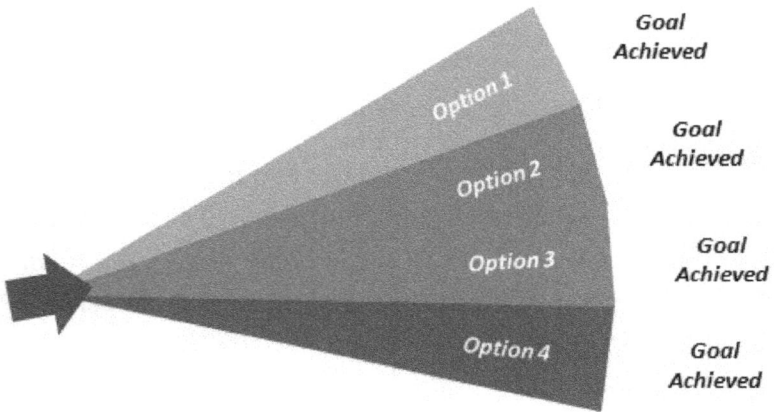

There are always other avenues, possibilities, opportunities when we start questioning and breaking down the walls we construct for ourselves and those around us. So…how might I accomplish my airplane goal with this new viewpoint? Just a few options for consideration…

1.) Create a business plan and purchase the plane via bank credit, with minimal down, as a business start-up to carry freight as a courier service. *Commercial insurance required, but no passenger issues.*

2.) I love seeing smiling faces, personally pay for the plane and operate a small sight-seeing charter company to defray the monthly costs. *(Minor passenger issues, but limited destination time tables or schedules to contend with on a daily basis.)*

3.) Pre-Sell airtime/flight time with local businesses. Use the signed time agreements as brokered/referral collateral to purchase the plane over time from plane's owner with no money out of pocket and minimal time investment from me.

4.) Search for someone who wants to start a skydiving academy, crop dusting service, or some other seasonal venture and purchase the plane together. Simply use it during the off-season for my personal use.

As ridiculous as these 4 examples might be, it serves the point that when you open your mind to the possibilities, opportunities present themselves. I'm positive that a fair number of you are already thinking about Options 5, 6, 7, & 8 that I haven't listed. The point is that our goals can be quashed before they ever take root if we allow "Stupid Rules" to cloud the issue. In all of my examples above, the hidden opportunity of actually making positive revenue from the plane would be missed by conventional wisdom. *Hey, a possible "Sliced Bread" moment...* Imagine taking something that you've always been told is an enormous cost, not justified unless you are "only happiest in the air", and turning it into a positive revenue stream in the long term.

Now, let's look at the flipside of this argument from the point of view of someone who might also be able to benefit by helping me achieve my "Airplane Goal."

1.) A local bank searching for new loan clients. *(Might be willing to entertain a high collateral business startup plan)*

2.) Local businesses needing quick service charter flights for freight, clients, employees at a lower cost and easier flight-plan options than regular commercial service. (Especially during hunting season to small towns in Texas)

3.) A current plane owner who is looking to bolster his business during hard times. (Debt relief, additional income, or succession/exit planning)

4.) A local investor who needs to invest loose capital to reduce annual tax liabilities or increase depreciation.


I used the "Airplane Goal" because it is a frivolous goal from my youth. It really doesn't matter what the goal is, there are always opportunities to succeed when you open your mind to the possibilities. And the simple exercise of uncovering hidden opportunities can lead you in a direction of helping others achieve their goals with you. Imagine the potential when you create a "Team of Allies" *(much more on this later in the book)*.


### *Aligning Goals can be magical:*

In my airplane personal goal above, I illustrated an example of finding or creating a business which was aligned with my personal goal of owning a plane. "How" they were aligned in the hypothetical was immaterial, the simple act of trying to align goals opened the doors to possibilities previously not considered.

In my career, it has amazed me how many businesses, managers, and corporations could actually positively intertwine their employees' personal goals with that of the company. These opportunities are too often missed in our structured, shareholder-value, quarterly-rush, or private ownership dividend way of thinking. If we truly stepped back and took an honest view, we might find that our personal goals really aren't that different than that of a basic company's goals.

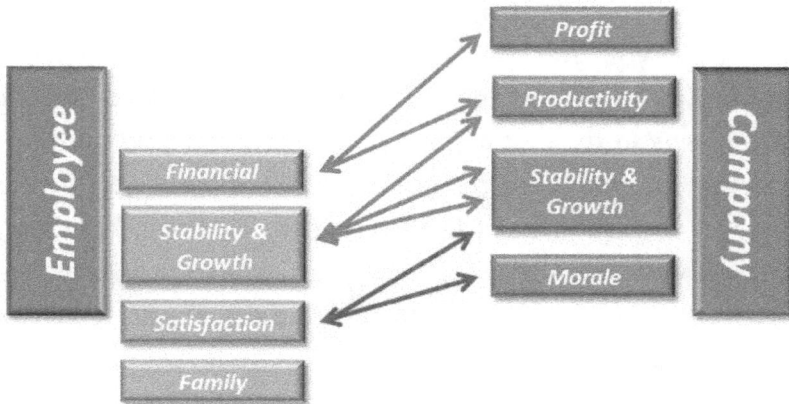

This is a generalization of course, but highlights an interesting point. You might think that they are competing goals, that they don't align, and we shouldn't waste time working to align them. You might say, *"Even in your own illustration, the boxes don't even line up."* We might view Company Profit as not relatable to our own lives, when in fact, we all have financial goals ourselves. They might be saving for a trip, new car, next month's mortgage, or simply new back-to-school clothes for the kids and not the Thousands or Millions of $$ per year that the company has targeted. Whatever your financial goal is, it is present.

Most companies want Profit, Productivity, Long-term Stability & Growth, and basically a happy/safe workforce. On the flip-side, most families want financial security, stability & growth/advancement, personal satisfaction (quality of life), and protection for their family members. These arrows point both ways. The company can help you achieve your personal goals and you can help the company achieve their ultimate goals. There are dozens of other main goals, thousands of variations, and sub-categories, but this basic illustration will suffice for our simple example.

You might be saying, "Adam, that's just Pie-in-the-Sky" jibber-jabber. Well is it? Have you ever shared the cost of a vacation or trip with a friend, spouse, or family member? *(assuming it was a trip or vacation you wanted to attend in the first place...don't kill my example thinking about the miserable trip you were forced into by "that" part of the family...)* Have you ever worked just a little harder or worked extra hours to stay in a little nicer hotel, go to just a little nicer restaurant for your anniversary, or work together just get household chores done a little faster to make extra time for a date night or spend extra time with your kids one weekend? These are all examples of goals aligning in our personal lives that can easily spill over into our work lives.

Now that we've tested how to think differently about frivolous airplane example, let's take a moment to review my old $100,000 annual goal for a less frivolous example to test how we could have intertwined a personal goal with that of the company's goals.

*For Example:*

Over the years, when I've managed commission-based sales representatives specifically, I would never hesitate to ask about a personal goal. For example, "Adam, you told me that you wanted to earn $100k annually by the time you were 24 years old. You are 20 years old now, which gives us 3 years to get you to that threshold." *(It doesn't matter if my goal would have been a Corvette, a plane, home with my family, or extra vacation time to travel abroad)* But for the sake of argument, let's stay with the $100k annual for this fictitious example.

If you start at $35k base, we will need to increase your book of business by 3x to exceed your goal and account for fluctuations/losses along the way. With a XX% sales $$

commission, you will need to be managing $XXX in annual sales for the company. That is an increase of roughly $XXX in sales. Over 3 years, your target would need to be $XXX+/- in new annual sales growth. *(Plug in any commission % or Sales Figures here, it is merely an example to show how I would present it to an employee)* The company, if their commission plan is sound, should stand to make profit on every new sales dollar I bring in the door, so it stands to reason that they would want me to sell as much as possible to increase their own profits. *As a manager, how can you help your team truly succeed without knowing what drives them?*

The illustration below highlights how we could simply intertwine Adam's Personal Goal to achieve 2 of the company's goals. Personal Finance to Company Profit & Company Productivity.

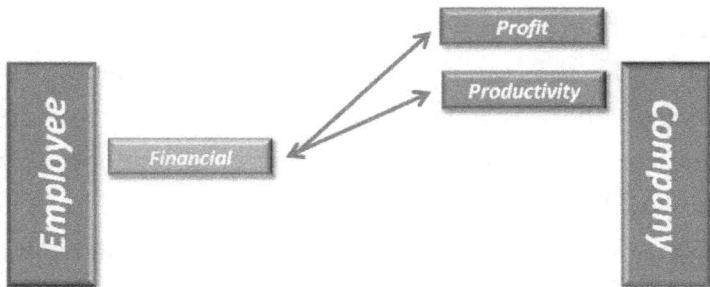

If I had been Adam's manager all those years ago, I would have taken a few minutes to highlight a few options for Adam. I would include our average customer attrition rate, look at the current new sales dollar averages from other Reps, *(Both of these items every manager should know and track)*, and build a simple timeline for Adam over a 36 month period to help him track *OUR* progress. Why 36 month time period? Two reasons — that was the timeframe he wanted to achieve the goal and because it also magically satisfies one of the company's goals at the same time – Stability & Growth over time.

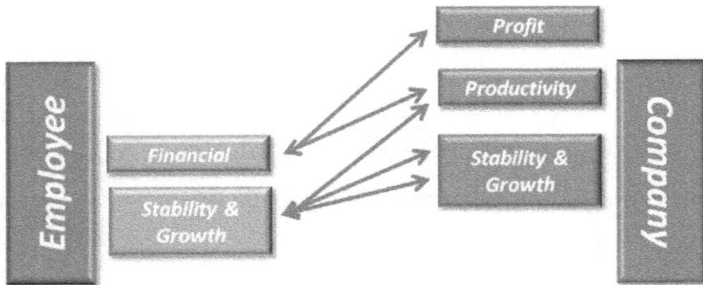

I would list the Company's base target for Adam on the chart, so that we could visually see how *OUR* new goal compared to the base goal & averages. Keep him positively motivated on the way to achieving *OUR* goal. It is now easier to help and motivate him along the way because we both have the same long-term target in mind. As a manager, there is nothing better than being able to pat someone on the back for minor accomplishments along the way as simple motivation to continue to push for success. Which, by the way, completes the Goal circle of Personal Satisfaction & Company Morale.

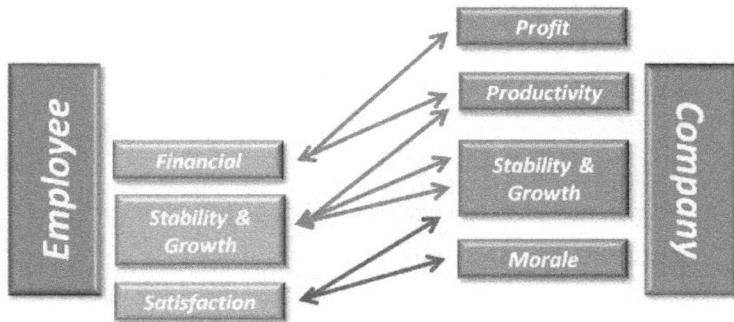

*What seems to get lost in the HR landscape today is that these types of motivational tools need not interfere with stated job duty goals. If the company's stated target was lower than the employee's stated goal to achieve, then anything above that would, in essence, highlight the employee's prowess as a top performer, right? Why would we ever want to take that drive and determination away from someone?*

So, what have we done here? Just by having the discussion about trying to align a single goal, we've successfully intertwined Adam's stated single personal financial goal with that of the company and were simultaneously able to align 3 other similar goals. We created a plan to help us both achieve *OUR* goals, created a bond with an employee that is deeper than a mere job, and perhaps, committed Adam to working with the company for years, even if other job offers came his way. All because we were both focused on the same overall goal. Now we have to go out, work hard, and try to achieve it.

As a manager, if you can intertwine your company goals into the personal goals of your team members, you begin to want to see them succeed. If you truly want to assist them in every way possible, the employees will be able to feel your support and honest willingness to help them achieve their personal goals.

What works for sales people works for truck drivers, operations managers, VP's, and families as well. Try to intertwine your team's personal goals with that of the company/group so that you can succeed together. Now that we've looked at a sample goal-alignment, allow me to give you an actual example of how it has worked for me in real life.

*Appointment setting:*

When I owned my insurance agency, I reached the point where I held a firm 95% closing rate. I was closing over 95% of my weekly calls and I was only limited by the available time in the week *(5 appointments per day from Tues-Fri – roughly 10-12 hours per day)*. So I brainstormed about how to reduce my office time and increase my sales time.

A thought occurred to me….hire and train Appointment Setters… These were people I could train to sell insurance for me as the years progressed, complete & submit necessary paperwork for me *(removing one of life's little personal frustrations for me)*, and reclaim additional time throughout the week to allow me to sell more plans with my additional time. Where do you find these people? You find college kids, still attending classes, who want to work part time and possibly start a career in the exciting world of insurance, of course. I say that in jest, but it is easier than you think when you have a solid plan, open mind, and are willing to sell yourself and a real opportunity.

I hired several appointment setters to start, built their compensation plan based upon my closing rate, as an incentive to set good appointments for me. I trained them how to make cold calls, provided their leads, and tracked their progress. I warned them that this process is arduous, however, it is much more difficult to set an appointment for someone else than it is for yourself. My closing rate dipped to 90% over time – less prep time to ensure every appointment was firm and with a solid prospect – but overall, only a 5% drop was well worth the additional calls and extra profit, even after paying my appointment setters.

My star performer was a single mother who had a young son at the time. We had honest conversations about her life goals when we began, and constantly along the way. I laid out the compensation plan I had designed, we discussed her immediate family needs, financial needs, and how we both felt that she would best succeed. She was personable, upbeat, could relate to mothers from personal experience in a way that I could not *(not being a single mother myself)*. She wanted a job that could turn into a career when she finished school that would still allow her freedom to spend time with her son, watch him grow and provide a stable income. She thought that pursuing a career as an insurance agent might provide that.

*Her Itemized Goals -*

1.) Work from home to provide care for her son.
2.) Work flexible hours around school & family.
3.) Be able to train with me to sell insurance and meet clients.
4.) Not have a pre-determined # of calls to make per day/week.

*Oh, the Stupid Rules I heard at the time — "No one ever hires appointment setters as an independent agent", "It won't work because they aren't licensed agents and cannot answer questions", "That just isn't the way it's done..."*

It wasn't long before she began to choke out my other appointment setters, filling my schedule and working on the upcoming week's schedule. The only real problem I encountered was that she was too good and there simply wasn't enough Adam time throughout the week. She exceeded even my own high expectations. It wasn't long before I toyed with the idea of selling their extra appointments to other agents *(at a tremendous mark-up)* — those same agents who said it would never work.

We were able to intertwine her personal goals with that of my own. For those of you in Human Resources, I will offer this disclaimer — her compensation plan, job duties, and overall program was exactly the same as my other team members. The difference was that she wanted to succeed, had strong goals in mind, and we were easily able to align our goals. She won, I won — we won together.

*Just a sideline smile for a moment — even so many years later as I still received small residual commission checks from time to time from those insurance plans sold so long ago, I had to laugh when filing our taxes and proudly presenting several small insurance 1099's to our CPA one year. One 1099 stood out and particularly puzzled him. It was for an annual commission totaling $14.99. The plan had been in force for so long that the commissions were literally melting away, but, for me, it wasn't about the money. I simply had to smile because I knew that the original plan was sold during my appointment setter period and I remembered hearing* *so many other agents and brokers at the time telling me how my plan would never work.*

My small goal of simply removing some of my daily paperwork frustrations and manufacturing additional time in the week blossomed into a full on staff of appointment setters, over-filling my calendar, and generating positive revenue even more than a decade later. *(Even as I write this, a smile forms on my face when I contemplate how one little short-term goal had such a tremendous impact for me.)*

### *There is more to achieving Goals than just crossing the Finish Line…*

History is littered with people, for whatever reason, who seemed destined to immediately itemize the single "Right Way" to achieve a goal or succeed in general. I constantly ask myself why this is. Sometimes, in our minds, we simply take the "path of least resistance" and fall in line with the old ways of completing a task to avoid the seemingly futile battle against the "Stupid Rules" in our daily lives. We've all done it and said to ourselves…"It's not worth the battle…" when confronted with obstacles in our path.

I have found, however, that more often than not, there is more than one "Right Way" to accomplish something, as we've illustrated several times in this book already. Life is ever-changing. Why would we not expect the old standard rules to change along with them?

I've made a lot of cold-calls in my life. I've made a lot of sales calls in my life. I've heard the word "No" so many times in my life, it's ridiculous. But through it all, I've learned things about myself. Such as how I respond to various types of people and how to interact with certain types of people. I've learned who seems to respond best to me and I've tried to determine why. I enjoy seeing the "light bulb come on" when someone opens their mind to a new possibility.  I enjoy testing & questioning the boundaries, pushing a limit or two, and finding a new way of doing something.  The challenge itself excites me and drives me to improve.

Allow me to give you a quick example I learned from years and years of cold calls about a personal goal being somewhat different than the "standard norm".  This outlook has worked for me for years through insurance, corporate sales, business startups, and even in my personal life *(My beloved wife will probably roll her beautiful eyes when she reads this...)* It's just become a natural part of who I am.  Try to create a little intrigue, be a little different, lead with Personability and a smile.

In point of fact, I began to ask myself a simple question…"Where am I going and what do I want to accomplish?" My ultimate long term goal was to build my book of business. How might I best accomplish that? Simply slogging through today's work? Or doing today's work, as well as making life easier for tomorrow's work at the same time? Hmm… now that's an interesting thought. I began to revise my short term daily goals.

When cold calling to fill my appointment calendar specifically, I would pick up the phone, call a number from a target list I had created *(sorted by industry, company size, total sales – whatever metric suited the occasion or product)*. I always tried to take great care of knowing who my target audience was and who I was ultimately trying to reach. *(I cannot stress how much frustration this has removed for me in the past)* Most of these prospects, I had never contacted before.  I have found that most sales people, as well as the customers they contact quite honestly, dislike cold calls because of the awkward nature, the perceived waste of time/lack of benefit, canned speeches and the low closing rates. *A lot of this is can be attributed to poor prospecting to start.*

If I had viewed the task of first-attempt cold-calls by the old standards, *(in other words, if I had been on someone's rigid program and someone had been tracking my appt / phone call closing rate, they might say that I wouldn't succeed in sales. That I didn't push hard enough or that I didn't follow their time-honored script.)* I knew that I never enjoyed being tied to a desk, making call after call, so I changed the game for myself to give me a brighter outlook. This translated into more positive completed calls per day, fewer overall calls needed, a warm follow up, and a better experience for the customer. Most importantly, it ultimately resulted in a better closing rate for me in the field. Field time is expensive time, especially when you're running your own business — office phone time and prep work are cheap by comparison.

**_The Call:_** *(from Recycling & Waste Disposal, but the product is less important than the process)*

*Adam:* "Who would I need to talk to about buying your old cardboard for recycling?" *(Variations abounded depending on my mood for the day, but always a smile, laugh, but always in a friendly tone.)*

*(Wait for the pause as the receptionist's head pondered such a ridiculous question)*

*Adam:* "I bet that's a question you get every day." (wait for their giggle — which ALWAYS came)

*(Their reply was almost always the same...almost every time...)*

*Receptionist:* "No, I can't say that's a question I get every day...I guess you would need to speak with Bill/Mary/Jane/John."

*Adam:* "Perfect, is he/she around?"

*(At this point, 80%+ of the time, I would be routed to their voicemail and I welcomed it. When I reached their voicemail, I would simply leave a concise, yet moderately mysterious message.)*

*Adam:* "Hi Bill/Mary/Jane/John, this is Adam with XYZ. The market is changing again and as an end-user of your materials, I simply wanted to give you a *quiet* update. You can reach me at (xxx) xxx-xxxx, again (xxx) xxx-xxxx. Thanks and I hope you're having a great day."

Strange you say? Because my goal was not to make the sale over the phone – my goal was to either generate a call back or provide myself a natural warm follow-up down the road *(easier work tomorrow)*. Any appointment, discussion with the MGR over the phone, or ultimate sale I could set up at this point is a bonus. Whether they ever listened to my message or not, I was now armed with vital info and had laid the groundwork for minor intrigue. *(Understand this – Insurance, Recycling, Waste, and Packaging are all exceedingly dull topics for most people...jazz it up and create a little fun for yourself).* Just from that basic seemingly "No-where" call, I now knew that the company was still in business, that they had a designated person who was in charge of their recycling, who that person was, and, most importantly, I was armed with an automatic follow up. Now, when I called back, I had the MGR's name..."Hi there, is Gary around?" Said with purpose and an aura of "essential business" we needed to discuss, the gatekeeper would usher me through directly to them.

There are many things *(especially administrative tasks)* in life that we don't like to do. Sitting at a desk making call after call is not something I would say that I particularly ever enjoyed. Changing how I achieved my goals changed my focus and my outlook. It made me happier, generated a better response with my customers, and ultimately fit my style better than that of the jackrabbit, hard-sell, push for the appointment, filling-a-daily-call-quota mentality.

It was important for me to remember my ultimate goal...My ultimate short-term goals were to sell as much as possible, generate a true bond with the customer/client, and build a lasting relationship for long-term growth. Looking back, I can appreciate how changing the cold-call game changed my outlook on making call after call and ultimately made my time in the field more productive.  So was I right? It might not fit into someone's rigid program, fit into their norm or standard method, or might even seem like extra work, but it worked for me.

I carry these lessons with me and as a manager, trainer, or simple employee, I have always simply tried to get someone to define our ultimate goal. Then, we can back-into the innumerable possible ways there are to achieve it. I've seen companies run through employees like AAA batteries, viewing them as interchangeable cogs, one person viewed as just the same as another. I've seen companies "Stack Rank" their employees as a motivational tool to highlight top performers, motivate mid-performers to reach the top, and quietly hint for lower performers to move on. I've seen companies set daily, weekly, monthly call targets for salespeople. All had their specific purposes, built on their "prior experiences", but it always seems that when I've questioned them, I was able to poke small holes in their reasoning.  Can we look at the bigger picture of what you are trying to accomplish?

For example, let's just look at a generic sales regimen. A very large financial service company, which will remain nameless, that I've had several dealings with over the years, put their incoming sales reps on a 1,000 cold calls per month program. It was a verified, tabulated, documented monthly regimen.  Their "Right Path" to success. They engrained in their incoming reps, most of which were brand new to the industry, that this was the call volume necessary to accomplish their goals based on the closing percentage of prior representatives. 1,000 monthly calls, 1% closing rate = 10 new clients per month. *My jaw dropped when I heard this.* I was in a similar industry – Insurance and held a 95% closing rate with way fewer calls. Was it their products, their training, their reps, their program? What was causing the exceedingly low closing percentage leading to the formation of this rigid program?

When I met with the Manager of their territory offices, I asked him about their individual goals for the reps. 10 new clients per month – a simple goal. *(It isn't lost on me that there are ancillary marketing benefits of having your company name spoken to 1,000 people per month, some of which don't care about the person making the call, but might do business with the company in the future based on name recognition, or that it is perceived to be a great way to weed out non-performers, etc – I get it).*

I asked what they would do if a new rep secured his 10 new clients on 100 calls. Would he have to complete, verify, and document the remaining 900 calls that month? With a charming smile, he simply responded, "They should want to keep making those calls, to start building for the future, etc, etc, etc." *(I had to snicker, because it sounded like something I might have said as a generic answer.)* The manager continued, "They should want to keep making those calls to build their book of business faster and get off of the base training stipend we provide as quickly as possible." Their hard and fast, 1,000 monthly call rule, was set in stone in their minds to justify their training bonus, stipend, and draw as the new reps built their book of business. In my mind, it was just an unnecessary "Stupid Rule" they had created for themselves.

Could they modify the program to create a positive motivational change for their incoming reps? Could they work on improving the dismal 1% closing rate and remove some of the rigid barriers from their team's daily lives? Why not? My mind spun with ideas as I met with this truly charismatic and confident manager touting his and his team's successes.

1.) Where are they getting their prospect lists? The phone book? Is it 1,000 "Good" calls or just 1,000 dialed numbers?
2.) How are they training their new reps? Are they only training about the product list and not about "How" to sell them?
3.) What was the turnover rate for reps? *(Insurance had been about 2 reps out of 10 survived in the long-term)*
4.) What is the company doing to help them - other than providing a desk, a phone, and a giant set of rules?

On, and on, and on questions ran through my mind. I was reminded of the Algebra equation we discussed in the beginning on this book:

$$X + Y = Z$$

$$Z = 10$$

Remember this? If Z = 10 (Stated Goal of new clients per month), they perceived 1,000 calls per month + Their Training = Their Goal. The quality of the individual rep and the quality of their training / products / territory / prospect lists and customer retention were all left completely out of the equation. *(Think about that statement for a moment... shocking, isn't it? But we make these assumptions every single day when we don't question the status quo.)* Take a person off the street, put them in a suit & get them licensed, make them call a ton of people every month, and we can hit our targets. It was all very clear to them, normal and secure - the standard they had grown accustomed to.

Ahh...the old dreaded "Numbers Game" adage. That, my friends, is what we call marketing or order-taking...not sales. Throw enough spaghetti on the wall and some of it is bound to stick. Get your name out there enough and someone will call. But I always wanted to know more... What was it about that single piece of spaghetti, that single advertisement/mail-out/flyer or call that worked? What went wrong with the other 990 calls per month? Let's review the root cause and we might find a better way to achieve or exceed our goals.

What was lost in this equation was that making 1,000 calls might work, but there could be innumerable ways to improve upon it for better long-term success. Is it really about the 1,000 calls or is it about something else? Were there 100 positive calls that led to the 10 new clients? What was different about the 100 calls?

Here are just a few pitfalls I've seen from this way of operating:

1.) Who is _your_ target audience? Can you define it?
2.) Where/How are they getting their prospect's contact info?
3.) Are they making "Good" calls? Solid prospects, decision-maker?
4.) Are they following a script? Are they asking the right questions?
5.) Do they endear themselves to the client? Does their personality shine during the conversation?
6.) How many of the 1,000 calls are follow-up "Warm" calls?
7.) Are they properly prepared to answer client questions?
8.) Did you, as the company, do anything to help bolster their success?

Remember my adopted motto? "The Customer only values/ trusts/ respects you as much as they _Feel_ you value/trust/respect them." *(See, I told you the words were interchangeable and you didn't believe me...)* If someone ever *feels* that they are part of the "Sales Numbers Game" then you instantly become one the generic "numbers" of random people calling them to get into their pocketbooks – not to provide a solution to their problems. This is especially true when you are trying to market a product based on "High Value" or of "High Importance" to them.

Another pitfall of these types of programs is that they always seem to make assumptions after the fact, as if to validate themselves. *"Well, look at Tim's success. He followed our 1,000 monthly call program and he is one of our top performers now." Or the flipside, "Billy didn't make his 1,000 calls this month and he missed his target. See, if he had followed our program, he would have been as successful as Tim."* Not everyone will be successful, regardless of the program, training, products, etc. Some will be successful in spite of the program. And then there's someone like me, for right or wrong, who sees it from the outside and would never want to be a pigeon-holed into the program in the first place.

Would I be successful there? Maybe. But I know that it would have driven me absolutely crazy along the way. If you are willing to commit to such a structured and rigid program, you must come to terms with the fact that you might not reach your company's, team's, or even your own full potential. You might drive away top performers before they even start, you might constrict someone's growth by funneling them into the "Right Path" as you define it.

Looking back, I truly wish I would have had the opportunity at the time to dive in and work with the manager on designing a new program, to help train their reps, re-aligning their goals from top to bottom, and helping them achieve those goals. But alas, at the time, I was in my own world, designing my own insurance agency and focused on my own growth goals. A missed opportunity, perhaps.

As I move forward into the business consulting world, these types of situations, programs, and methods are firmly engrained all around us.

Think about the structured programs in your life, for your team, in your company. What changes would you make, if you had the opportunity? What seemingly "Stupid Rules" must be satisfied or followed, but have had little bearing on whether you accomplish your goals? Was it simply the 1,000 calls you made or something else entirely?

### _Help others reach their goals and you might just reach yours:_

I might be a dreamer, but I am also a realist. Some goals are not as easily aligned. For an employee whose stated goal is to travel abroad, spend more time with their family, or flexible hours, the company might not be able to incorporate it as easily. Some people like the security of having a "job" and are not focused on "career". There is nothing wrong with this. Some people are happy working in the same position, the same hours, and the same desk for decades because their hopes, dreams, and goals are focused away from the company, either with family, retirement planning, or simply saving for next year's vacation. That isn't to say that we cannot try align their personal goals with that of the company and, quite possibly, the attempt to align a goal might lead us in a positive direction we hadn't considered before.

In every endeavor I undertake, I try to ask myself a simple question. What do we truly need to accomplish? For example, while managing truck drivers, I found very quickly that all of my drivers had different focuses, different interests, varying personalities, and different aspirations, even though some of them came from the same walk of life or career path. Some were what I lovingly called 'hour-eaters' _(those people who would work 20 hours in a day if I could let them)_. They liked what they did and they liked earning overtime pay. Others valued their family time and knowing that they would be off work at a regular time to attend to children and other various personal tasks. Some liked knowing they had a stable job with steady work and some highly valued being a part of a team.

Listening, acknowledging and adjusting as you work with your team, in my mind, is a large key to success. As I asked questions, talked with them individually and in the group, worked closely with them all, I gained tremendous insight into their personal situations. *Sales 101 – Yield the floor and allow the customer to speak...Listen quietly. (On the flipside, as an employee, I always tried to learn about my supervisors to determine what traits they valued in me, what traits they valued in others, and how they viewed our goals. My own process of trying to align my goals and highlight my personal traits they valued with that of my supervisor.)* Without ever making a formal declaration, we were able to simply, slowly, and systematically adjust their scheduled daily/weekly routes to provide the motivation that each individual enjoyed. Leaving a certain driver's schedule as closely to the same hours every day (mileage and traffic dependent), loading other's schedules heavier to quietly motivate them to push harder to complete more daily loads, working around their personal schedules *(allowing them to occasionally start earlier when they needed to end their day a little earlier)*, and simply offering volunteer-first holidays as a first-come-first-get holiday pay bonus.

My goal was a happy, well-motivated, efficient, profitable team – safety first, but always striving to improve, removing old frustrations and helping resolve problems. I wanted my team protected and stable, I wanted my customers serviced on time and with a smile. Their individual goals were varied, but I think we were able to align most of our goals to the benefit of the team. When I left the company, I received several calls from the same drivers asking me to take them with me in my future endeavors and still keep in contact with them to this day. For me personally, there was no better compliment I could have received from my team. The old "Stupid Rule" of "They are just truck drivers", "They are all the same", "They just want to milk the clock", etc didn't hold true for me...

### *The Goal Ripple Effect:*

Everyone has done this when they were a kid – thrown a rock into a pond or puddle to see the splash. I've thrown and skipped dozens of rocks into dozens of rivers, ponds, puddles, and lakes in my life. That isn't meant as a ridiculous brag...although I'd love to say that I was an expert rock-skipper. *(I think my personal best was a measly 4-5 skips in a row)*. But a thought occurred to me as I began to write this book. There is a strong correlation to throwing a rock into a still pond or fast-moving river and aligning your team's or family's goals. *I can hear you now..."Oh...he's going to launch into one of his existential metaphors of life and motivation..."* I won't offer anything so dramatic - just a simple thought to ponder.

What happens when you throw a stone into a still pond? First a splash, then the ripples move outward to each shore, depending on the size of the stone and the depth of the pond. What happens when you throw a stone into a fast moving river or stream? Just a splash and the river continues to move along with only a minor interruption.

I once heard a statement – *"As a manager, don't worry if you don't have time to lead your team in the direction you want. Your team will be busy leading it in their own directions."* That's a scary thought. Yet I've seen repeated time and time again with various companies. One thing I've learned over the years in my career is that if your team is moving in the same direction with goals aligned and focused ahead, when issues or problems arise, you might see a splash, but it doesn't interrupt your overall flow. You are the fast-moving river. The team quickly reassembles and moves onward. The same is true with customers – aligning their goals with yours, building the relationship of mutual trust and value. You can quickly move forward from a service issue, payment issue, or product issue when everyone knows that you are focused in the same direction.

The peace of still pond, however, is easily interrupted by even the slightest little issue. Everyone focuses on the splash and can begin to move in opposite directions to escape the ripples. If the ripples are strong enough, co-workers might search for other jobs, customers might search for other vendors, friends might lessen contact, or your team might lose cohesion. I've seen this happen more times than I care to admit from companies.

Remember my adopted motto of "An Employee only trusts/values/respects the company as much as they _Feel_ the company trusts/values/respects them? I've seen resignations or terminations of employees, when handled poorly, begin an unwanted employee exodus within a corporation or division. I've seen simple projects, which could have created a strong sense of teamwork among co-workers, devolve into bickering and turmoil. I've seen small little arguments between spouses or family members begin to create a major rift. I wasn't always in a position to help, and some things appear destined or unavoidable as times change and people grow apart. But the optimist in me continues to say…"Just maybe, had they been able to focus in the same direction toward a common goal, this could have been avoided." "Maybe if they would have just listened to each other, they could have resolved a small problem before it became an apparently unsolvable mess."

Ask yourself a question…in your career, are you a part of a fast-moving river or wading in a still pond?

Throughout my career, I have begun to grow uncomfortable when I "felt" like I was on a team who was transitioning from a fast moving river into a still pond. For example, I worked for a company with declining morale from an overall lack of clear direction and leadership focus. At the time, I could feel the waves around me, I could feel coworkers moving in opposite directions, I could sense the strength of the ripples building as seemingly larger rocks were thrown into our metaphorical pond. So, as an employee (not as a manager), I created the following employee survey and forwarded it to our upper Management as a suggestion. It was October of that year and we were just beginning our 4th quarter, so I felt it was the perfect opportunity for upper management to engage our employees, gather their insights, gather thoughts & their ideas, in the attempt to align our goals as we began the next year. *The following is the exact document I presented (names removed):*

# Process Improvement & Team Building

## Improvement Ideas for the upcoming year

As we finish this year, we have a great opportunity to re-build our commitment to our (Company/Division) Team moving into the next year. We value all of our employees' thoughts and ideas and we thought it would be prudent to allow all of our key team members to voice their opinions on specific ideas to improve their daily work lives. Since our team members all depend on one another to perform certain job functions, this will provide a great opportunity to express your thoughts on how we might be able to streamline some processes or remove growth barriers next year. We have built a strong team of forward-thinkers and your ideas can help in many areas, such as: Process Improvement, Information Flow, Team Building Opportunities, Morale Boosters, Motivation Steps, and individual job role improvements. ***Strong Team = Strong Growth***

Please take a few minutes over the next few weeks to itemize some of your ideas to improve items which cause frustration, slow down progress, create extra work, or otherwise de-motivate you.

> ***Process Improvement:*** (Changes to Forms/Documents, Ways to improve Communication, Speed up Work Flow, Remove added or double work, reduce errors, etc)
>
> 1.)
>
> 2.)
>
> 3.)

***Communication:*** (Ways you believe we can achieve better communication amongst our group)

1.)

2.)

3.)


***Team Building, Morale & Motivational Steps:*** (Ways you believe we can create a stronger bond between our team members, improve the work environment, and increase growth)

1.)

2.)

3.)


***Individual Job Roles:*** (Specific ideas to improve individual job functions in your daily work life)

1.)

2.)

3.)

When creating this survey, my goal was simple. Create an outlet for people to confidently voice their opinion and work toward the long-term improvement goals. You might recognize that I purposely left off questions about "How do you feel about the company?", "Do you feel valued?" "How are we doing?" etc.

This survey was not about the past, it was about our future... "How do you think we can improve?" "What ideas do you have?" "How can we help you?"  This very subtle distinction makes all the difference in the world in my opinion.  I was coming from the point of view that "We want to Improve...Help us Improve..." *It is no different in sales. It isn't what YOU as the customer can do for us or what we THINK we can do for you...it's all about what we CAN do together and how you FEEL we can help YOU.*

If you step back and look carefully, you might recognize that each section of this simple team survey mirrors and combines individual chapters in this book. I actually created this survey well in advance of authoring this book. Now that's an interesting thought...

1.) **Process Improvement** – *Let's question the old ways we have performed tasks, discuss options or changes, and resist falling into the "Stupid Rule" of "we've always done it that way..." Continually strive for improvement.*

2.) **Communication** – *How can we learn & combine the different personality types, different thought processes, and different personal experiences of our team? Learn, listen, grow...*

3.) **Team Building, Morale & Motivational Steps** – *Continually working to align our goals and provide an outlet for creative* *suggestions & solutions. <u>Fast moving rivers move in the single direction - forward.</u>*

4.) ***Individual Job Roles*** *- "Build your team of allies" (more in a later chapter). Refer back to the Round Pen or finding Carrollton on the map. Even if I had previously held their specific position at some point during my career, it would have been in a different time, with my own thought processes guiding me. We might have been asked to complete the same task, but we all "prefer" to operate differently. <u>Minor Positive Changes – Huge Impact.</u>*

It was quietly dismissed and was not adopted by our upper Management for wide release to our division. At the time, management believed that it would create grief, turmoil, and unreal expectations – ultimately that each employee would request things that would cost the company money or that they would ask for increased pay. *("Stupid Rules")* My view was that it allowed team members to voice their honest opinions, feel that their views were truly appreciated and foster the "Team of Allies" that I had strived so hard to create. Several months later when I was promoted and my team began to grow, I was given permission to present it to my team. Knowing how corporate managements operate from time to time, it was probably a "taste of his own medicine" tactic. I pressed onward with management support and gave it to my individual team members without a moment's hesitation.

When I received them back from my team, the team members I worked closely with daily, I was truly surprised and encouraged by some of their responses. Almost every idea they presented was positive and could easily be incorporated into our routine. Bulletin board for updates/changes, simple ideas to increase efficiency, contact sheet for out-of-the-norm occurrences to reduce confusion or downtime, minor changes to their daily forms (larger font, different color scheme that is easier to read, etc).  More than anything else, it showed that I valued their opinions, got everyone talking & thinking about improvements, gave them a little ownership of the situation, and moved the team forward.  *I have always thought that the "carrot on a stick" trick only works in the short term – just until everyone realizes that they will never actually reach the carrot….a real trail of breadcrumbs when your team can actually taste the improvements along way works best in the long run.*

It is important to understand that just because you might not be able to incorporate many of the ideas (extra vacation time or increased pay), it provides an excellent boost of motivation to incorporate some simple changes that cause minor frustrations in the daily lives of your team. I've heard from numerous people since then that it was very dangerous to engage your employees in such a manner.  "What if the results come back poorly? What if it reflected poorly on management? What if, What if, What if?" *My internal response – If you don't ask the question, then you probably don't want to work on a solution...*

One specific result from this survey was a driver who mentioned "Truck Yard Congestion" as a topic of improvement. I discussed the topic several times with this driver after the survey so that I could listen to some of his specific ideas. I assembled a small team committee comprised of employees from Operations, Sales, & Maintenance – the 3 departments who all had a stake in improvements from that particular facility which had the issue.  I elected this driver to be a "Yard Captain" *(my designated driver representative to work with Operations and Maintenance to design an improvement program).* It all sounds bureaucratic, but trust me when I tell you, that the sparkle in everyone's eyes as they discussed their ideas, easily bridged the gap between departments, and openly discussed their own issues paved the way for vast immediate improvements.  *We were simply aligning everyone's goals...*

Such a simple thing garnered such a tremendous result in improved morale and outlook on the future. Varying ideas were floated, discussion points raised, and most importantly – it focused not only my team, but other teams in the company toward a small, common aligned goal. People began to believe that if we could work together on this little project, then we could work together on larger projects as well. What had been a still pond of frustration and inefficiency could become the fast-moving river of a lean, productive, safe working environment. The "Stupid Rules" of "We've always done it this way", "You won't get any cooperation from them", or the ever-maddening, "It won't work…" objections were replaced with "Sure, let's try it and see what happens."

## Goals, The Risk, and the Details...

---

We've all heard this adage before, "The Devil's in the details..." This is very true, on an assembly line, fast-moving conveyor, or simply balancing your checkbook, pennies add up and small details can snowball into major disasters. But that really isn't the point – helping those around you to view their own big picture and seeing beyond the next step, is the atmosphere I strive to create for those around me.

The simple fact of the matter is that, I have learned throughout most of my career in daily sales, "Focusing on too many Details can kill a Deal for a customer." I try very diligently to paint the broad view for people around me, not in an effort to hide pertinent information or to be sneaky, but in an effort to allow their dreams, thoughts, and wishes to filter unabated through their minds – to see the possible potential rather than focus on all of the possible pitfalls or obstacles. And what I have found, is that generally there are simple solutions to most problems you might encounter, being open to alternate possibilities allows us to make minor adjustments to still accomplish our goals, and generally create ancillary opportunities along the way... opportunities that we had never considered before.

Life is filled with opportunities not seized because of the "Stupid Rules" we just accept at face value from conventional wisdom, or the instinct to hold back until every detail is ironed out and discussed. That isn't to say that we should never look-before-we-leap, but when you look back on your successes or perceived failures in life, how many times has a small detail _actually_ derailed you in your quest to achieve your overall goal?

Let's face facts. We've all had a customer who didn't turn out to be as profitable as we thought they would have been.  A team member that didn't pan out the way you expected or a project that went over-budget. Think about one of those times in your life.  Was it poor planning or did the parameters change after the fact? Did the customer unexpectedly lose a contract lowering their overall volume? Did the team member not pan out because a circumstance in their personal life changed (divorce, new child, spouse's job change, etc)?  Did the project go over-budget because of an unforeseen obstacle you encountered (tree roots where you planned to dig, material delays, weather, etc)? Was it truly because you missed a major item, a lot of little details, or did the circumstances simply change along the way? _We will circle back to details later._

How many opportunities have you missed? Have you ever caught yourself saying, "Looking back, I wish I would have tried that"? I know I have. _Even as the author of this book, I can count numerous opportunities in my life that I wish I would have tried._ But it isn't about regrets...it is about where we go from here.

## My Risk Assessment Template:

In an effort to focus my thoughts and keep the ultimate goal as my target, I developed a simple "Risk Assessment Template" (*if you want to brand it with a catchy title*) years ago and still use it today. Many times, this can be done mentally, quickly, and without much effort. It can be done in a family setting, group setting, business setting, or alone in your career or personal life.

I have tried to teach this simple concept to many people over the years when we discuss a new project, new way of performing a task, or streamlining old/new processes. The applications are limitless and the labels can change depending on the application, but the overall concept is simple. Time and time again, when I present this concept to people, light bulbs flash in their minds, smiles appear on their faces, the speed of their speech increases, and they begin to discuss opportunities/benefits that I/We hadn't considered before.

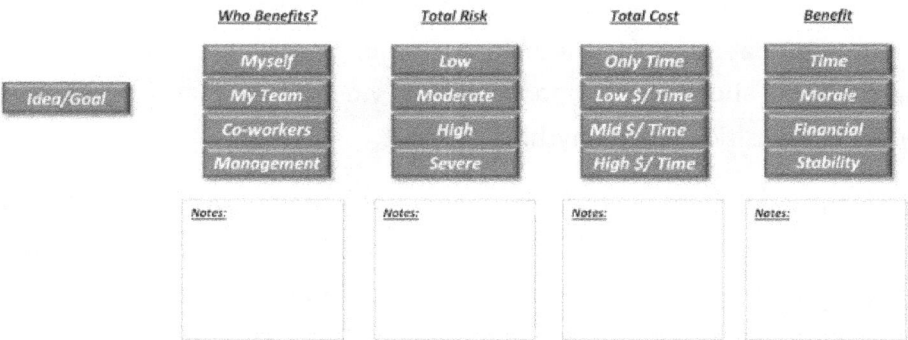

| | Who Benefits? | Total Risk | Total Cost | Benefit |
|---|---|---|---|---|
| **Idea/Goal** | Myself | Low | Only Time | Time |
| | My Team | Moderate | Low $/ Time | Morale |
| | Co-workers | High | Mid $/ Time | Financial |
| | Management | Severe | High $/ Time | Stability |
| | Notes: | Notes: | Notes: | Notes: |

1.) Define the problem/task first and then identify your solution (Idea & Goal). *It's not always a problem to be solved, sometimes, it's just thinking differently about "How" we accomplish a task.*

2.) Who stands to benefit?

3.) What are the total foreseeable risks & the total foreseeable costs?

4.) What is the Net Benefit you hope to achieve?


Try to remember….*and I cannot stress this concept enough to people…* If you are doing/creating/building a **_NEW_** Task/Product/Process, why would you let the **_OLD_** "Stupid Rules" cloud your vision? You were already halfway there…The sheer fact that you are doing something completely *NEW* should reinforce the fact that a tired argument of "We've always done it this way…" should not truly apply.

Allow me to refer back to an example we discussed earlier in the book. The new Transportation Dispatch System and new Logistics Clerk position. The company had never had a true dispatch system before. It simply wasn't viewed as "needed" the way we had operated before. Send a driver to the next customer, try to piece together a route sheet for the next day, wait for the next customer to call and write them on a paper Call-in sheet. This had bothered me for years and years, but I wasn't in a position to do anything about it.

The old guard was stalwart in their views of, "We've always done it this way, and 'a system' will cost too much money." *Perhaps they were right, in a way, at the time.* Purchasing an available dispatch system, sending someone for training, managing it, learning it, and being able to glean anything useful from it might not have achieved a targeted goal. They might have been able to justify or argue against it and been satisfied with their result. The simple fact of the matter was that as long as customers got serviced, improving the way we dispatched/managed trucks was not a goal at all, so anything along that line of thinking, in and of itself, couldn't possibly achieve a goal that didn't exist.

So what happened? It was neglected for years, it was not a priority, we sputtered along as we had always done. As the Sales Manager, I just did the best I could to keep customers happy and grow without accurate driver ETA's, missed hauls, changing priorities and grumpy drivers. Until...a sudden transition was needed.   When I took over the transportation management, I had to piece together several months of history, page after page of call-in sheets, in an effort to simply to try to assemble some kind of regular customer service schedule.  Now, I wasn't given any goals at the time either...I could have plugged away the same we had always done, working from day to day, adjusting when necessary and trying to keep our heads above water, but that just isn't me or my style.  *If we are going to do it...we are going to do it well, and do it better tomorrow than we did today.*

*The Problem/Issues –*

1.) No standardized processes
2.) No back-up in case I was out (travel, vacation, weekends, etc)
3.) Lack of historical data
4.) No Stability during transitions

*My Big Picture Goals –*

1.) Happy Team (carrying them through the transition smoothly)
2.) Efficiency & Productivity
3.) Profitability
4.) Stability & Growth
5.) Historical Data for Review

I stepped back, reviewed the issues as I perceived them, thought about my goals – "What do I want to accomplish?", I performed my little Risk Assessment exercise, and began brainstorming my solutions.

I think we need a real dispatch system of some kind to accomplish my goals. *(Actually, there were dozens of options that could help me accomplish these simple goals. But as we have covered "opening our minds to possibilities" earlier in the book, my focus here is to highlight a chosen option and walk you through the exercise.)* If the dispatch system helps me achieve my goal, then I can move on to the next step. How? What options to I have? Who will this benefit? What is the cost?

*What options do I have?*

1.) I probably won't be able to get approval to "Buy" a dispatch system. *(Not that I would really want to but a ready-made one anyway. Personally, I love building things like this and challenging myself...strange for a person "Lacking in Detail" I know...)* – *Agreed...Build it myself.*

2.) Since we've never had one, the options for "How" I design it are completely open. Who's to say I'm wrong/right? I'm really only limited to the programs I personally know and ones approved by corporate. Shared databases allow queries, form entry, multiple users, special reports, etc. – *Agreed... Build it in a shared Database*

3.) What main items do I want to be able to track, forecast, review, etc? Times, dates, drivers, customers, miles, hours, etc. – *Agreed – Flexibility & Ease of use*

| Dispatch System | Who Benefits? | Total Risk | Total Cost | Benefit |
|---|---|---|---|---|
| | Myself | Low | Only Time | Time |
| | My Team | Moderate | Low $/ Time | Morale |
| | Co-workers | High | Mid $/ Time | Financial |
| | Management | Severe | High $/ Time | Stability |
| | Notes: | Notes: | Notes: | Notes: |

So, in short order, I have defined what I perceived to be a problem, itemized my main initial goals, postulated a possible ways to achieve those goals, and quickly filtered my thoughts through my Risk Assessment template.

1.) **Who Benefits?** Me, My Team, Co-workers with easier data, Management, and potentially – all of our customers (*more on that later*).

2.) **What's the risk?** Low to Moderate. Loss of time, missed customer service, lag-time of the start-up or errors in the database. Well within my risk tolerances based on who all stands to benefit and the total cost.

3.) **What's the cost?** We already have Microsoft Office with Access on our computers. No cost there. Just a little of my time on nights and a weekend. Well worth the cost for me for the potential time savings, personal frustration and possible improvement along the way.

4.) **What's the benefit?** We could potentially save time through better routing, boost the morale of my new team (better info, better forecast of scheduling, fewer in-day changes), increased profitability through productivity and efficiencies, increased stability of having a baseline system in place during an absence (vacation, transition, etc).

Alright. I've decided that I am building my own transportation dispatch system, I know the base items I want to incorporate, know the cost of time I am willing to invest, and I've highlighted the potential benefits. Now the real work begins...

I imported our customer list *(after several late night reviews / updates / revisions)* and started listing all of the individual items I would be able to track. I met with a few of my counterparts in Operations and Accounting to present the base system and show them all of the items we would be able to track to determine how they could best benefit from the system. I asked the initial questions of "What do they actually need from the new system." But then I took it a step further and asked them "What they _Wanted_ from the new system." *(Attempting to satisfy someone's "Want" is a base tenet of my personability definition.)* Simply stated, it is much easier to open peoples' minds to possibilities when you can inspire them to think about how they can also personally benefit from your endeavor. Not to help yourself, but to help them – as you will read when we discuss "Building a Team of Allies" later in the book.

*Side note: This is not just a "more flies with honey than vinegar" sort of statement. It is deeper than that – I didn't need their approval to build the system, since it was basically a system used only for myself and they still could have benefited from my data. I didn't need their immediate help to build the system. I wasn't asking for any favors and using honey as a peace offering. (Although it never hurts to store a favor or two in reserve along the way.) The point of genuinely attempting to satisfy a "Want" for someone is that when you open their mind and ideas start to flow (from their point of view), additional opportunities can be discovered.*

You can imagine all of the minor objections, the "Stupid Rules" of "You can't do that," "It won't work," "What if this and detail that". All of the normal things you would expect to hear when you try something different and people see it for the first time. I nodded in agreement as each department rattled off items they needed to be included for their reports. Then I simply smiled when they realized that the system could actually generate their reports _for_ them...the light bulb went off in their heads. They simply hadn't considered that possibility before.

I mentioned earlier in my illustration and detail about the Risk Assessment template for the dispatch system that customers would also benefit from this. When I originally brainstormed the system, although I had worked in database programs before, I had not thought about the idea that we could email customized reports directly to a customer directly from the system. Office Managers in different facilities in our division could access the system (via a shared corporate drive already in place) to print their own custom reports for their customers. An entire world of benefits was bestowed before us...benefits that I didn't even think about when I started the endeavor.

Ok..I know what you're thinking to yourself. Adam, there are much better programs to use for that. Why didn't you set up FTP and allow customers to email directly onto and access the schedule? You've built websites for several companies, why didn't you build a website? Why didn't you search for a free-ware program still in Beta testing to use as your base system? Why, why, why? I love it...See, I told you in the beginning of the book that opening your eyes to possibilities and questioning perceptions was easier than you think. I'd be willing to bet, that as you're thinking to yourself of all the ways I could have done it better, that not once has a

"Stupid Rule" clouded your thoughts. Hence the essence of this book. When you start asking "Why Not?" and "How can we best accomplish our goals?" the things that used to hold us back seem small in comparison to what we can achieve.


### *The Devil's in the Details:*

Let's have a little conversation about Details as they pertain to my Risk Assessment template. I've talked about details quite a bit in this book so far...that personality tests might label me as "Lacking in Detail" or that people might perceive me a glossing over them. I've posed the question of "How often have little details actually derailed a goal of yours or a project" and was it really the details or an unforeseen change along the way that was truly the culprit.

From my experience, most people view a Benefit-to-Risk chart like this:

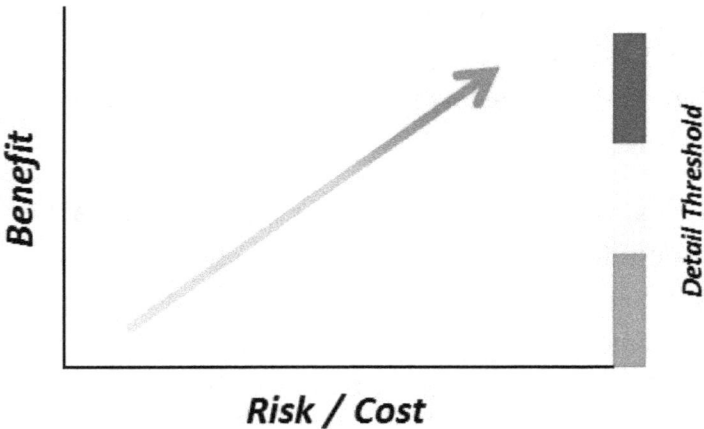

It is viewed as a simple linear line of how when the Benefit Increases the Risk/Cost also Increases. The conventional wisdom being that it is difficult to get a major benefit from something with very little risk or cost. The

Detail Threshold color-band on the right hand side represents the amount of importance we place on the individual details. More simply put, as the benefits increase, typically so do the costs and risks, hence the importance on focusing on all of the minor details all along the way. I mean, if you could get a major benefit from something without any risk/cost, why aren't you already doing it? *(Funny how no one ever seems to question the minor details then. Except when their cynical side takes over and it "seems too good to be true.")* Please don't tell me a "Stupid Rule" is holding you back...

Let's just get to the heart of the matter. It seems to me that everyone's definition of an Important Detail varies – just as their definition of Risk does. Just try it, if you don't believe me. Pick something you perceive as a minor detail you can overlook and someone will argue the point with you. *(My apologies to my wonderful Mother...I'm about to tell a story from my childhood – please forgive me.)*

When I was growing up, my sister and I would often receive a small slice of cheese from a block along with our sandwich in our lunch bags. A perfect rectangle slice was great. But when my sister or I ever received a slightly misshapen slice of cheese (i.e. a corner missing or a small chunk out of the side eerily not present), we knew exactly what had occurred. A small patch of mold had grown on the surface of the cheese and my mother, not wanting to be wasteful, merely cut off the surface mold and packed the slice in our lunch. HUGE detail to me...insignificant to her. *I joke about this because it is still a topic of laughter during family gatherings anytime a block of cheese is present...checking for misshapen pieces. My wife grins at me because she will cut mold off cheese, her mother does, her family does, my mother still does. My aversion is simply that I'm allergic to penicillin and won't go near it...whether it would be fine or not.*

Now, remember me overlooking a benefit package while interviewing, simply choosing to wait to see it listed on their offer letter? To some people this is a major part of the decision to change jobs, where for me, it was not a big factor at the time. The fact is that every situation, person, viewpoint is different. We all define "Details" and "Risk" differently. We all view different items with varying importance – all based upon our background, experiences, current situation, and current goals. It might have been viewed as a huge detail to some or a major source of risk to others, where to me, I was simply willing to wait and review it later.

We simply cannot see every possible outcome in the end (those unforeseen changes along the way), but when we step back and focus on our goal, alternate ways to get there, and ultimately what we want to accomplish, we might just reduce our overall risk and simultaneously open the door for ancillary benefits.

### *Turning an Olive into a "Sliced Bread" Moment:*

*(Why is it always about food with this guy?)*

Remember the old story of the airline CEO who discovered that one fewer olive on their in-flight salads could save the company tens of thousands of dollars per year....Would anyone really notice that there was one fewer olive? *(Probably not if the story had never gotten out).* Conversely, a clever person might point out that one more olive added to the salad could have tremendously cut into the company's profits. You'll say, Adam, that proves the point that small details matter tremendously. And I wouldn't argue that fact. But let's say, for the sake of argument *(since most of us aren't CEO's of an airline),* that it was an olive company rather than an airline for a moment. One fewer olive in the jar rather than on an in-flight salad.

My "Sliced Bread" moment every time I've heard this tired old story is simply the following: My contention was that all the focus was on the one fewer olive and no focus was given to whether the olives were actually good, how well their marketing campaign worked, where other improvements could have been made, and on and on and on. Tens of thousands of dollars per year could simply represent one manager's compensation, or one more sales contract with another grocery chain. What about printing the label in another language to sell in ethnic grocery stores to instantly expand your market? What about changing out an old piece of equipment, purchasing lower-cost lye or filtering & reusing the brine? Am I alone here? Am I the only person who hears a story like that referenced over and over and no one ever brings up an alternate view? The only thing I've ever heard about this story is that customers are upset getting less and being charged the same money. Yet it is touted as the ultimate success story of "Details add up to huge impacts."

### *The Process*

I will grant you that my mind might operate differently than most, and I'm willing to accept that. But when I have made presentations, performed training, or brought groups together to "white board" an idea, I tend to focus on the End Target/Goal and work backwards. I have found that opening my eyes to the alternate possibilities tends to answer many of the initial questions I, or my team, might have had – and provide better results.

Let's take the dispatch system example to allow me to explain my thought process. Start with identifying the problem you hope to resolve and then you can form your initial goals...

**_Goal_** - Happy Team, Efficiency, Productivity, Profitability, Stability

**_Brainstorm_** - How do I / we best accomplish my / our targeted Goal? What experience can I draw upon? What have I done in the past that has worked? What have others done that has worked?

**_Beneficiaries_** – Myself, Co-workers, My Team, Management

**_Needs/Wants_** – Track-able, Scale-able, Adjustable, Reviewable, Flexible, Ease of use

**_Options_** – What possibilities/options do I have? What is the Risk/Benefit of each? Build my own Transportation Dispatch System, Purchase a transportation system, Print & Save daily route sheets and simply enter the finished data each day for tracking *(Blah...)*, Search for a free-ware system rather than purchasing one, outsource the transportation management, and on and on and on.

**_Agreed Upon Idea_** – Build our own system to our own specs.

Ok...so what about the olive company? Let's say the olive fiasco saved the company $50,000 annually for our example.  How could the olive company accomplish the same goal in different ways? *Watch this...subtle change coming...* A simple change in "how" they interpreted their Goal.

**_Goal_** – Rather than "Save the Company $50,000 per year", change the goal to "Generate an additional $50,000 Annual Profit". *(I didn't say "cut costs" by $50,000 per year because that would pigeon-hole us into only*

*looking at one side of the accounting ledger. Now wouldn't it?)* Subtle "detail" to be sure, but this one actually does make all the difference in the world – at least to me. *Look at the bigger picture of what you are trying to accomplish before narrowing your focus.*

With the slight revision in how the olive company "stated" their goal, an entire world of opportunities could present themselves. Both sides of the accounting ledger could now work for them. Most companies do this intrinsically, always looking to grow and cut costs, but I rarely, if ever, see a Goal listed which incorporates both sides. Most goals I see are relegated to only one side of the accounting ledger.

What areas of your business or personal life can you review? Is there a sliced bread or olive moment waiting to be discovered? What are the risks of trying and what are some potential benefits? What initiative or project are you facing in your business life? Is it simply a quarterly goal? Monthly goal? Is it adding a new employee or, heaven-forbid, downsizing or transitioning?

# Part 6

# Building a
# Team of Allies

---

Who surrounds you in your daily life? Are they Allies or Competitors? It doesn't matter if you're a manager, parent, or a college student just starting your life's journey. Do you foster an atmosphere of cooperation, trust and helpfulness? Do you inspire those around you to achieve their goals? Do they inspire you to achieve yours?

You secretly know how you view and feel about the people around you *(secretly assigning Duck Types to them)* ...but here is a possibly unsettling thought...how do the people around you view you? If you're in sales – how do your customers view you? If you're a manager – how do your employees view you?

People's opinions about you can be formed when you least expect it. *I'm sure many of you have formed opinions about me, my thoughts and views, or how I must annoy my beloved wife from time to time.* In the

118

previous chapters, we discussed Aligning Goals, Motivation & "Personability", the types of people we are, and discovering a "Sliced Bread" opportunity for ourselves. Let's start the process of melding them together.

Please don't take this as a "sneaky" or "subversive" tactic or heading. Building a team of allies in my opinion is as crucial to achieving a goal as setting a goal is in the first place. We've all heard the old phrase "Goals are deceptive – the un-aimed arrow never misses…" And, while it might be true that flinging an arrow willy-nilly might never miss a target that it wasn't aiming for, I choose to think differently about that proverb *(as you might have guessed)*. The arrow might just injure someone around you on the quest for their goal. Just think about that for a minute… When our goals aren't aligned, when we aren't working together, when we aren't fostering a sense of teamwork or building our team of allies, we all essentially become competitors.

Remember the fast-moving river vs the still pond comparison for earlier in the book? I worked to help a company once that had everyone moving in their own direction. Morale was low, everyone practiced "covering their backsides" just waiting for the other shoe to drop – waiting for the next round of bad news or major course-correction. I told them this phrase at the time and still believe it whole-heartedly today – it is just one simple thought.

*A Team is a group of people working together for a common goal. Factions are individuals or small groups working towards their own goals. You can't succeed as a Team of Factions…*

Oh, we've heard the adage "the enemy of my enemy is my friend." That might work when fighting against marauders, but uneasy truces never work in the long run.

## Leadership is more than Steering the Ship:

Some managers might be reading this and thinking to themselves, "I need to get my team focused in my direction. I'll push out anyone who doesn't think *My Way*. I'll build my team of allies in my own likeness and we will all be happier – We will all work to build *My* legacy together." However, I cannot stress enough.....***Please do not get caught in this trap.*** This is not my point at all... The key errant thought in the statements above is I/Me/My.

Just a simple word of guidance that I've learned from years of wrong-steps in my career and life – some lessons are very hard-learned – when it becomes about Me, it is never about You. *Remember my adopted motto of: The Employee only Values the company as much as they Feel the company Values them?*

Building a team of Allies is always about the forward march of people focused on the team, focused on Our goals. I use the word "We" all the time. Even when I am speaking just about myself. *(I've had more than a few people ask about the frog in my pocket over the years...some of you might chuckle and catch that reference)* But when the goal is inclusion, how can you include someone when you are only speaking about yourself? Subtle item, to be sure, but it makes all the difference in the world.

I met with a consultant acquaintance of mine years ago and he told me an interesting story. It is Business 101 & Consulting 101, but somehow many managers/companies have missed this connection. Take your business, any business, and this theory will apply:

Take all of your managers (low-mid-upper) away for 3 days. What will happen? The general consensus (the most responded answer) is that 90% of the work will still get done. That isn't to say that managers aren't needed or necessary or to diminish their contribution. It is simply viewed that 90% of the day-to-day work is carried out by employees who aren't managers. Simple concept.

Now, take all of your non-management employees away for 3 days. What will happen? The general consensus is that either the world will end or 10-25% of the work will get done. But overall, the business will suffer in a horrible way.

Leadership seems to be akin to being a captain on a boat. It always seems to strike me as odd when I encounter someone in a leadership position who feels that they have one hand firmly on the throttle, the other hand firmly on the wheel and feel like they are in complete control of the ship. Seemingly, because everyone is tethered to their post, completely at the whims of the captain without any other options. I mean, after all, would you rather swim or just take orders and work on the boat? Remember, life and business is not a submarine and it isn't the US Navy. Your people have other options. *As a quick sideline, I have actually heard this phrase – I was stunned to hear it at the time and still stunned to re-cap it now – "(This Person) is too loyal to ever leave the company..." This phrase was uttered less than a month before that "Loyal" person resigned and left the company...* In this instance, the company & management viewed themselves as the ship/submarine, misguided about the employee's goals, mood, circumstances and confidently striding forward with the Manager's hand on the wheel, leading them confidently directly into the rocks ahead.

Building a team of allies is not a difficult undertaking. But we need to remember, the Captain's hand on the throttle or hand on the wheel is completely meaningless if the crew isn't going to respond, or by the consulting example before, if they are absent completely. Turn the wheel all you want, but if the motor isn't running, the ship isn't going to turn.

We all seem to have this romantic notion of a proud, brave, John Wayne leadership type – gruff & tough exterior, holding firm in the headwinds of change, stalwart in his decisions, and unyielding in the driving rains of adversity...proudly leading his men to safety. I mean, it worked in the movies, right?

My Way

**Goal Achieved**

This narrow mindset is the same type of linear view towards leadership that we've discussed in interpreting and not aligning goals. Might you achieve your goals? Possibly. Might you exceed your goals? Possibly. But might you also hinder your efforts, alienate those around you, build teams of factions against you, create a mutiny, distrust or disloyalty in the long run? Might you steam right by the hidden gems or additional opportunities along the way? I have always thought so. More importantly, I've seen it repeated time and time again. Everyone nods their heads in a meeting with the manager and then whispers to their own team of allies as they leave the meeting.

Just as we open our minds to the possibilities around us, take a step back, and rethink your "Leadership" strategy. Could we have turned those pennies into dollars? Could we have built a stronger team? Could we have opened more doors along the way? What "Sliced Bread" moments have we missed by being so focused on the bread knife that we are caught blindsided by the possibility of not needing the knife any longer when the automatic bread slicer is invented? What about the people in our organization that might have seen it coming, but were too timid to mention anything because of my stern hand? Are you mad at them because they didn't tell you? Did you foster an atmosphere that lent itself to discussing opportunities?

This is all very dramatic...*and I don't really do dramatic*...but it all simply serves to focus our attention that when you look at the picture from a different perspective – US as a team rather than ME as the leader, it can change your viewpoint on potential missed opportunities.

Perhaps I view it a little differently than most. I'm willing to accept that. But let's assume that you managed or owned a bread knife company all those years ago before the invention of the automatic bread slicer. The company's overall goals were typical – Profit %, Longevity & Stability, and Building the best bread knife known to man. You, as the leader, built a team of allies, working towards aligned goals – your profits were good, your team was motivated/productive/happy, and the company's bread knife was one of the best around. When the automatic bread slicer is invented and slice bread hit the market, what do you do?

As the leader, do you face headstrong into the winds of change, unrelenting against the tidal wave of cheap sliced bread rushing onto the market and still work to produce the singularly best bread knife known to man? *Don't wait to build a team of allies until you feel it is absolutely needed. How many of the employees of the knife company were already buying sliced bread for their breakfast table and wondering about the future of the company?*

Start slowly changing your viewpoint now to be ready for the next tidal wave that *always* comes. Let's take the same automatic bread slicer example from the Team of Allies viewpoint. If the original goal was to produce the best bread knife on the market, there is nothing to say you still can't produce that. But what if you had been discussing, researching, opening your eyes to possibilities all along the way beforehand? Hmmm...

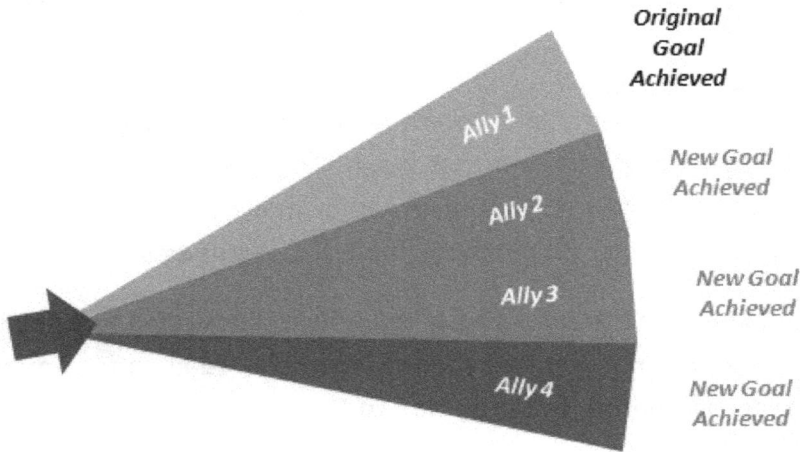

Original Goal Achieved

New Goal Achieved

New Goal Achieved

New Goal Achieved

Ally 1
Ally 2
Ally 3
Ally 4

The company can still produce the best bread knife (Original Goal), but with your existing equipment, perhaps you could market a revised butter knife (for jams, jellies, spreads and butters) – specifically marketed for sliced bread? Or the best cheese knife set on the market? "From the people who brought you the best bread knife on the market – now the best Cheese knife to match." What about joint marketing with the artisan baker who would not ever use an automatic bread slicer for their special holiday loaves? Ever thought about making cutting boards or expanding into flatware? What about chef's knives for the professional market? The point is, that while one person might come up with a few ideas, you are all thinking about other possibilities at this very moment. That's the entire concept behind building a Team of Allies as a leader. Building the goodwill that only comes, not from someone working towards Your goal, but working towards Our goals.

I've spoken quite a bit from the leadership point of view. But don't lose sight of the fact that, as an employee (not in management), as a sibling, as a friend, as co-worker, these principles still hold true. As an employee specifically, without any team members beneath you, think about how you can build your team of allies with your peers and with your manager. You are all a team and all heading in the same direction, for good or bad, after all. Listening, learning, assisting, discussing, reviewing and building these relationships vertically and horizontally are an essential tenant of building your Team of Allies.


### *Too many cooks in the kitchen:*

I know what you might be thinking. Adam, that is a ridiculous example. What company only makes 1 item and isn't diversified? The answer is lots of them...I see it every day and hear from businesses every day that "This is what we do and this is all we do..." I won't list any names of the companies, but think about the numerous photography film conglomerates that have fallen by the wayside in the digital age. Now, very few people even own a single digital camera...they simply use their phones for social media posts. What good is a digital camera if I can't post the pictures instantly on Facebook? Just think...people were slicing their own bread for thousands of years as well....

Yet I still encounter resistance to new ideas with the same "Stupid Rule" of "Too many cooks in the kitchen." *(Yes, another food analogy)* The idea being that everyone adding their own ingredients into a single sauce will spoil the result. Too many competing flavors. While this may be true in the course of action, it is all too often used as an excuse for not building a team of allies to start. While multiple people adding spices or ingredients into the sauce while it is cooking might spoil the result, it is more likely that everyone's goals for the finished sauce were not aligned in the beginning.

How about this for an example of leadership? It is Tuesday. You, as the head chef or leader of a restaurant, are serving thick cut pork chops for dinner on Friday night as your special. You assemble your team of allies (sous chefs or cooks) and relay the main goal – The best pork chops we've ever made, with the best complimentary sides we've ever made. You lay out a simple plan. Each of your team members can work on their own, together or individually, to design a total menu incorporating your main ingredient. On Wednesday, those who participate will present their idea and test-cook a sample for a group tasting. Everyone will decide on the best items and the menu/shopping list/agenda for Friday can be set. *I love the simple type of camaraderie these types of events can create – smiles, laughs, sense of teamwork and assistance toward a common goal.*

Allowing all of the team members a little freedom to play, test, design, try their hand at leadership, giving them a chance to shine, providing a little sense of ownership, doesn't diminish your role as the leader. It enhances the experience and knowledge of your team. Now, they aren't cooking at the same time in the same sauce. They are trialing an idea and testing themselves toward the common goal, based on their own background and experiences. Someone might say – Applesauce glaze, because it is the standard for pork chops. Others might say curry to jazz up "normal", others might add a stuffing or choose to fry it rather than grill it...

*This is no different than the simple 4<sup>th</sup> quarter survey I created to align goals for the following year...simply on a smaller scale. And no different than the motivational Post-It Notes I gave to team members along the way. It is all about building a team of allies...*

So what's the absolute worst that could happen? Some managers and companies might say that it breeds competition amongst the team. That it could de-motivate the individual whose items weren't chosen. That it could foster dissention in the ranks, so to speak. Possibly. But I find that when options are given to allow members to test, trial, and play a little, all options are put on the table to discussion (and in this example – tasting), then a better overall result can be attained. But you see, a strange positive side-effect of this type of leadership is that, although one of your team member's ideas might not be great for this Friday's Pork Chop Special, it might be perfect for next week's Chicken special...don't miss a chance at finding a hidden opportunity by not taking the little chances along the way to Build a Team of Allies.

In management, sales, or parenting – these little opportunities are all around us. In this example, the main course was chosen by the head chef or "Team Leader" (either by choice, religion, demographics, sale price on pork, etc). The main goal didn't change – make the best pork chops we've ever made. How we arrived at the goal is the only thing that changed in the process and a world of opportunities opened up for future growth.

Sometimes we are handed Pork Chops as the Friday Special (new goals from corporate, auto bread slicers introduced to the market, opportunity for a new large account, or the loss of a large account). That is inevitable. What we should try to instill in people around us is the idea that the positive results from positive motivation can far outweigh any of the potential risks.


### *Risk vs The Team of Allies:*

Let's face it...risk is all around us. We talked about aligning goals, building a team of allies through subtle leadership changes, and about fostering an atmosphere of cooperation rather than creating silos that divide us into our own tasks. Let's address the risk portion of the debate.

| Idea/Goal | Who Benefits? | Total Risk | Total Cost | Benefit |
|-----------|---------------|------------|------------|---------|
|  | Myself | Low | Only Time | Time |
|  | My Team | Moderate | Low $/ Time | Morale |
|  | Co-workers | High | Mid $/ Time | Financial |
|  | Management | Severe | High $/ Time | Stability |
|  | Notes: | Notes: | Notes: | Notes: |

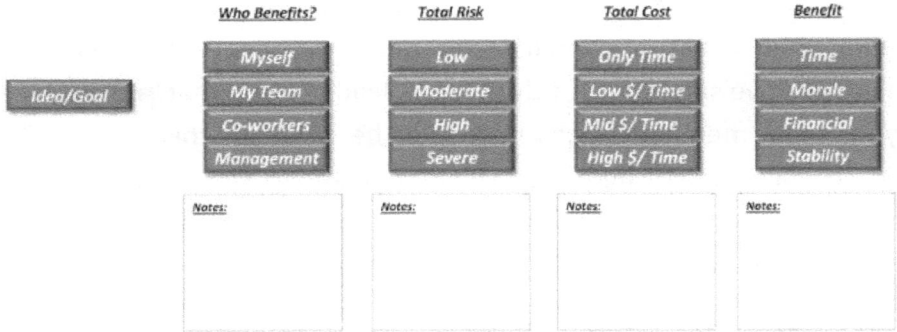

Remember my Risk Assessment tool from earlier in the book? You might have realized that the word "Benefit" appears in two headings while "Risk" only appears in one. "Why", you ask? Because when I weigh a potential risk, I want to look at the Total Risk as one item, but look at all of the possible benefits separately (Beneficiaries and Itemized Benefits). This isn't about pushing to sell the idea or overlooking the "details" we've discussed in earlier chapters. For most things in life that we attempt or endeavors we undertake, as the number of benefits or beneficiaries increase, the overall individual risk of the idea, project, task, can actually decrease.

I find that nothing drives success for a Team of Allies more than ownership, or a personal stake, in the project / idea / task. Does this mean that you have to give a financial reward for everything? No. Ownership or Personal Stake in most cases is simply the sense that people "feel" they helped, that they got a chance to stir the pot or lend a hand, foster an idea or help remove an obstacle. Anyone can nay-say...the team of allies builds together.

Let's take the Friday Pork Chop Special example again. There are thousands of objections that nay-sayers could voice:

Risk - A curry sauce is more expensive or time consuming than applesauce – we would have to charge more.

*Potential Solution - Did we ever list a target price on our Goal? So if we need to charge $19.99 rather than $18.99, will that drive away customers?*

*Potential Solution - Do both sauces mix well with the side-dishes for the special? Can we offer both at different price points? Would that actually help us sell more by offering two choices to customers?*

*Potential Solution – If we make both sauces, does the curry sauce keep well to be used over the weekend for other dishes? Can we use the applesauce for other dishes? Perhaps an apple dessert of some kind and maybe curry veggies on Saturday?*

As you look at a risk for most things we encounter, you will find, when you open your mind, potential benefits can abound. The apple dessert might be a huge hit. The curry veggies might pair perfectly with Saturday's special. Would you have found these opportunities if you hadn't brought the team of allies together, fostered their ideas, and allowed their minds to experiment with possibilities? So what happens when we uncover hidden potentials? The Overall Risk of the idea is diminished. If you can realize 25% of your goal from each part of an idea as a bare minimum, then you increase your chances of exceeding your goals as you continue to add ancillary benefits to the equation. The Team of Allies, all with a small stake in the process, can each provide a small piece of the equation to reduce the overall risk from only focusing on one "Right Way" to achieve a goal. If everyone is truly aligned, the goal/total risk can be easily separated amongst the group. It might ultimately be your pocketbook on the risk line as the owner, but it can also be your pocketbook, employee morale, longevity, and company stability that reaps the benefits…

One of my favorite everyday items are Post-It Notes *(as you probably could have imagined from my numerous references to them in the book)*. Did you ever hear or read about how they were invented? 3M adopted a sanctioned bootlegging policy to allow its employees to test and develop new ideas using existing 3M products or other works-in-progress. Obviously, 3M would reap the benefits of any final product which made it to market, but that isn't the point. Art Fry used a reusable adhesive developed by another 3M scientist, simply to keep his bookmark firmly attached in his church hymnal, so the story goes. As it was developed, even the distinctive yellow paper was chosen/used simply as a function of the extra paper they had in the facility at the time for another project.

So was there a risk for 3M allowing their employees to play with up to 15% of their time on a pet project? Of course. But I would be willing to bet that most of those people also spent countless hours in their personal life thinking about the idea at night while trying to get to sleep, in the shower in the morning, on their commute to work, in their garage at night… That's how we all are. We focus on the things that interest us. Be it cars, projects, family, etc. I build business plans, develop products, brainstorm ideas, work independently on other's marketing plans, work with charities, try to hone my skills, test my ideas and expand my personal horizons – oh, and author this book. Are there risks? Of course, but the overall benefits can far outweigh them.

What chances do you have to reduce your overall risk by building, motivating, and fostering a Team of Allies around you? What innovations can they bring to your company's table? What future issues do they see from their perspective that you might not see from yours? How many benefits can you discover from a simple brainstorming session when you allow your team to dream a little? How many of your company's employees think about work improvements or frustrations in their off-time? Is it about how to help or improve the company or is it about the negatives of the company? What daily risks could they reduce with simple solutions?

*More things in your life were born from someone testing an idea than you might realize. The dreamer in me wonders what innovations, improvements, or exciting projects are just around the corner for all of our businesses, if we could simply tear away some of the "Stupid Rules" of days gone by and risk to look into "what might be…"*

### *The Team that gets stronger every day:*

We discussed in a previous chapter the concept of Motivation and Personability. I highlighted a few of the things that I do every day to try to inspire those around me. From a simple text message in the morning to brighten their day, to a brainstorming meeting to solve a specific issue or achieve a specific short term goal. Building a team of allies is a conscious decision and choice we make and renew every day. "Turning upside-down ducks right side up."

Sometimes we are reminded how much we impact the people around us. Not long ago, I was confronted with an electrical panel in our house shorting out and almost catching on fire. It was simply old and with a few abnormally cold winters recently, the strain from the furnace was simply too much. Marching onward, waiting for an electrician to complete the replacement of the panel, we went without electricity in our house for a few days. One morning, I was speaking to one of my daily work vendors, joking about the quickly-worsening mood of my beloved wife, when the vendor made an offer which still makes me smile when I think about it.

"We have an extra bedroom if you both need a place to stay for a few days."

This vendor was a person I had only known for a few months at the time. The offer wasn't made to curry corporate favor, extend a contract, or grow their business with me. It was simply made because there was an honest connection between us that went deeper than just a mere vendor relationship. They truly wanted to help in a time of need. I don't tell this story now as a, "Hey, look at how great I am..." point of view. I tell it simply as a function of building a team of allies and the realization of my definition of personability.

Take a look at your team - whether you are a parent, manager, business owner, or employee. Is your team getting stronger every day or being slowly whittled away? *That isn't to say – is everyone happy every day...* What can you do to assist them? How can you inspire your team or allow them to challenge themselves? If you're a manager, how long has it been since you reviewed your team members' current resumes? What experiences or accomplishments have they made in their personal lives that you both could draw upon now under different circumstances? What do they like to do and what do they excel at? In meeting a company years ago, I took an independent look at their salespeoples' books of business. (I have done this for myself several times over the years, just to take a peek at how my books of business have changed over the years) I itemized it by industry segment and size of customer. What I have found every time I have done this exercise for a company is that each salesperson will have a predominant segment of their customers in a single industry or classification *(paper manufacturing was always my highest percentage of customers – simply because I grew up in the industry, worked in the industry, and had experience and contacts in that industry).* Some salespeople come from automotive, food manufacturing, distribution, construction, etc and have those specific classifications as their predominant customer types. There is nothing wrong with this. I work to create a stronger team by not by highlighting how "Weak" someone is in one particular area, but how "Strong" you are in your particular area.

It surprises me how few companies perform these types of exercises. Perhaps it is the belief that without the atmosphere of cooperation in place, or the feeling that the atmosphere of cooperation is being built, this can be a difficult task. To me, it is a wonderful way to start the process of building a stronger team of allies. A great way to start building the common feelings of teamwork by combining knowledge to tag-team prospects, sharing proposals and experiences, sharing successes & discussing similar failures, and finding commonality between industries. You might find, just as the olive company could have, that a simple marketing change or slight adjustment in how their goal is stated, could open a whole new world of opportunities for you.

For example, I had a large customer whom I had worked with for years. I had always stayed away from a large portion of their business because no one in our organization had experience with those types of products. *(Actually, I had been introduced to them through a very large prospect of mine. It is interesting that I was never able to transition this prospect into a customer – long story for another day, but I was still able to get a referral from their upper management to get in the door to work with another company who became a long-time customer of mine).* But back to my original customer - their product mix was branded by management as too high risk for too little reward... until...a new person joined our team. His background was in their specific niche industry and we were able to slowly start growing our business and deepen our relationship with my customer. Simply by being able to draw upon someone's background and aligning our goals, the Team of Allies grew that day...He and I had a common bond in this account – and it was greatly beneficial to the overall company as well.

What works in sales works in accounting, operations, maintenance, management, finance – from top to bottom. Knowing your team, drawing upon them, inspiring them, and motivating them is the key. Building a team of allies is something we work on every day, but building a team that can get stronger every day and deepen their relationship is where the real magic can happen.

Remember my example of electing a driver to be the Yard Captain? It was a small project, but all of these little things along the way provide us an opportunity to build a stronger team, with aligned goals, if we simply allow ourselves to look at the opportunities. One small change, providing a little ownership for the Yard Captain didn't de-motivate the other drivers because it wasn't a large personal focus of theirs. But it did inspire Maintenance and Operations to join the conversation and jump onboard our team of allies towards accomplishing our goal.

This type of open mindset does not require huge gestures of additional responsibility or monetary compensation (as the "Stupid Rules" would lead us to believe – "They won't do that unless you offer a bonus", etc), it simply requires the belief and determination to work together toward a brighter and more prosperous collective future… Imagine what you can accomplish tomorrow. ***People Buy Into a Team***

# Part 7:

## Try not to equate Fame with Success

Allow me to ask a few questions. There's no need to answer them aloud *(I probably wouldn't be able to hear you through your e-reader or the pages of this book anyway)*, or even write down any answers, simply think about them and we will circle back at the end of this chapter.

1.) Do you feel that you are successful? Are you happy?

2.) Who is a "Successful" person you know that you respect and why?

3.) What is one personal goal you have achieved that makes you the most proud? What personal or career goal(s) are you striving for currently? What is driving you?

4.) When was the last time you were inspired? Who inspired you?

135

To frame our discussion, let's refer to Merriam-Webster for the "accepted" definition of **_Success_**:

a. the fact of getting or achieving wealth, respect, or fame

b. the correct or desired result of an attempt

c. someone or something that is successful : a person or thing that succeeds

Just as we have discussed the definitions of Rules, Stupid Rules, Personability, and how we all define details and risk differently, let's start the discussion about the definition of "Successful." Is there a secret committee who meets annually in a classified location to determine what constitutes success? Or regarding your specific level of successfulness? Who decides if you are successful or not?

If you need a more clear picture of how engrained the idea of Fame & Wealth = Success, simply look at the first part of the accepted definition of Success. "Achieving Wealth, Respect, or Fame". Books, television, and anyone on the street would agreed that the late Steve Jobs, Bill Gates, Mark Cuban, or Jerry Jones are highly successful people. They are heralded as "Outliers" or "Mavericks" *(I thought you would like that, Mark)*. I wouldn't disagree with those points, except to mention the fact that there are countless people in your daily lives that are successful in their own right / their own way.

The simple fact is that most people in life will not be, for what most people would consider, famous. By the accepted definition, most people in life will not be, for what most people would consider, successful either. Fame aside, it is a shame that we would simply gloss over the daily success stories of regular people in our daily lives without ever acknowledging them, learning from them, or embracing their achievements.

Just as I might think differently about how to set or achieve a goal, how I search for opportunities, and how I constantly question "Why not?", you might guess that I view success slightly differently as well. Just for fun, below is a list of people you've probably never heard of before, but we probably all use the descendants of their products or ideas in our weekly lives. All of these people started with an idea. They invented their respective product, changed or revised an existing product, or simply saw an opportunity to seize and ran with it.

Alan McMasters – Electric Toaster – 1893

Otto Frederick Rohwedder – Bread Slicer – Fully Working Machine 1928

John W. Hammes  – Garbage Disposal – Patented in 1935

Art Fry through 3M– Post-It Notes – 1974

William Howard Livens – Electric Dishwasher – 1924

*Don't worry if you haven't heard of these people before. Neither had I until I researched some of the products. Most of these people have been lost in anonymity over the years as their products have become ubiquitous in our daily lives.*

I have been fortunate enough in my life to meet some people I would consider highly successful and have been afforded the opportunity to glean information and advice from them over the years. You probably wouldn't recognize their names, even if I did list them here. In my youth, I was introduced to some of these people and received a unique insight into their personal lives and history. Some of them became a few of my mentors throughout adolescence and into adulthood. One of them introduced me to Insurance all those years ago and started me on the journey I'm still following today – finding my own way in this world.

In the very beginning of this book, we discussed the different personality types and how we all operate a little differently and our varying views of problems, solutions, details and risk. Some of us simply have the goal of being wealthy or famous, I will grant you that. But some of us have the goal of being healthy and safe. Some of us have goals of conquering the business world and being a market leader – some just want to start their own small business. We should all understand that there is nothing inherently wrong with any of these goals. What might seem unreasonable to some, might be the ultimate comfort zone or sole driving force for others. The trick is, as we have discussed, to discuss and share these goals, try to help others accomplish their goals in the quest to accomplish your own.

Let's look at a Gold Medal Olympic athlete for example - the pinnacle of success in their field for that particular moment. That is, until the next round of Olympic competition. These athletes become household names during the Olympic season and can be quickly forgotten afterwards. Does that diminish their successes, simply because the fame subsides? None of these people simply "stumbled" into a Gold Medal. It took a goal vision, years of hard work, dedication and the desire to succeed. Is it any less of a success for the people whose goal was to simply compete and represent their country in the Olympic Games? We get so focused on their Q-Score for advertising, and their wealth and fame that we tend to lose sight of the bigger picture.

My beloved wife, whom I love dearly, worked diligently through college to finish early, started her career, went back to school to earn her MBA while working full time. I could not be more proud of her for this. Her goal was to prepare herself for a corporate career in HR. She accomplished two main personal goals. I would call her a success in my book, regardless of how the world might view her career path or goals.

My career path was exceedingly different than hers. My goals were different than hers, my upbringing was different, and my personality is different. *(Now you're really wondering...this sales guy with his wild ideas, strange personality, and distaste for "Stupid Rules" – married a very structured, rule-orientated HR person? Hey, opposites can attract.)*

The point is, just as we open our eyes to the hidden opportunities all around us (as we define a goal and how we might best accomplish it), let's open our eyes to the myriad of success stories all around us – from the people we encounter every day. As you work to inspire those around you, speak with them about their goals, you can uncover so many opportunities and helpful insights into achieving your own goals.

### *Plumbers, Mothers, & Teachers:*

Back to Algebra for a moment. The same student who wrote a letter to World Book Encyclopedia was also the same student who was confronted with, what I perceived to be, yet another "Stupid Rule" when I entered the Algebra II classroom. As we started the year, our teacher explained her grading system that she had used for decades. All of the Tests and Quizzes comprised 80% of your total grade for the year. The remaining 20% was for what she deemed as "Effort Points". *(Whether you completed the daily homework assignments, paid attention in class, etc)*. It did not take me long to notice a trend...the homework assignments were "practice" for the daily quizzes. The answers to the homework questions she assigned were in the back of the book to allow you to "check" your work. *To me...."Stupid Rule" – it amounted to mere busy work if you understood the concept of the problems and how to solve them...*

We debated the merits of her grading system throughout that year. Not in a confrontational way, mind you, but simply from the standpoint of revising the system to allow for flexibility. I pleaded my case, she pleaded hers and we moved forward under her "firm" grading system. Throughout the year, I completed no *(or very few)* homework assignments. I didn't value them, as I paid attention in class, took notes, and was able to pass every quiz and test she administered. By my calculations, I should have had an "A" in the class based on her system of Tests and Quizzes. I had scored A's on all the quizzes and tests, but my report card reflected a "C" due to the missing 20% for "Effort". She had been teaching for decades at that time, using the same grading system for decades based on her experience. *(Trust me, I understand her concept of trying to provide extra credit for those students struggling & just trying to get through her class).* I simply questioned why I would be "unjustly" penalized for not completing needless busy work if I could pass the quizzes and tests. Wasn't that the main Goal? Learn the concepts of Algebra and problem solving? Prove that you can pass the tests along the way? Prove that you've built a firm foundation for future math endeavors?

I am happy to report that at the end of the year, I was awarded "most" of the 20% Effort and received an "A" as a final grade on my report card. Perhaps she felt sorry for me or perhaps I was able to be a dent in the Rule Armor at a young age. Regardless of how or why, I think back fondly on that very special teacher.

What was her goal? Her goal was to teach. Her goal was to expand the minds of her students, prepare them for life, and impart knowledge on the young minds of tomorrow. *(Her goal could have also been to get me out of her classroom as quietly as possible...I'm willing to accept that...)* But regardless of her actual goals, I would call her a success in my book. Not because I gained a benefit of her rule-change or exception, but because she made a lasting impression on me.

Teachers might never be famous or wealthy, but how many of your teacher's names do you remember all these years later? What lessons do you still remember? If their goal was to teach you, where they successful and why?

What about the small business owner, farmer, rancher, mother or father? What were their goals? I've known many farmers and ranchers in my life growing up in Texas, that you could pass on the street or in the coffee shop and never give a second glance. Many of them that I've spoken to, have, what the outside world might consider to be, meager goals – keep the family farm intact, raise a family, be self-sufficient or leave a legacy for their children. What's wrong with that? Nothing in my book. The world needs farmers & ranchers. We need mothers and fathers. We need teachers, plumbers, police officers and firefighters. We need to stop thinking that just because some of the people are not rich and famous that they aren't successful either. Or that their goals are not important. What about the employee who never aspires to be a manager? Are they branded as not being a "Team Player" or a "Bobbing Duck" simply because their career goals are not centered on management?

We have discussed aligning goals quite a bit in this book because I truly believe it gives us the best chance to achieve our mutual goals...our chance to be successful in our own ways. But I've seen too often the measurement of someone else's success or failure viewed through the lens of our own goals or experiences. Remember that sometimes the competition isn't crazy after all...Take the single mother who was my star appointment setter. We were able to align her goals and both of us benefited.

Who is on your team and what are their goals? Looking from a slightly different perspective now, who around you would you consider to be successful? Has your perception changed?


### *Are you successful? Are you Happy?*

Wealth & Fame aside, would you consider yourself successful? More importantly, would you consider yourself happy? I sincerely hope that you've gotten a few moments of laughter and happiness from reading this book. I have found, and am reminded seemingly every day, that personal success and happiness can go hand in hand. Now, that's a matter of interpretation. Does happiness help breed success or does success ultimately breed happiness? *Oh...the unanswered existential generic questions posed in self-help or business books the world over...*

Through all of the examples in this book, thoughts, tips and tricks, I hope that the simple thought that I am a happy person shines through. I learned when I was a radio DJ for a short time during college, and later in my sales and management career it was confirmed time and time again to me, that smiling while talking lends itself to a better response. Although you cannot see my smile through the text of this book, I hope that optimism and the thirst for possibilities is an underlying current you can feel. I have found that I am happiest when I am assisting / training / teaching, building, growing, and working towards a goal. Essentially dreaming and working to realize the dream. What drives you? Where you are happiest?

As you recall, and put into practice, some of the ideas in this book, I'd like for you to keep one important thought in your mind. What makes me the happiest or feel the most satisfied? We can talk about setting goals and aligning them, building a team of allies, personality types, sales & management tips and tricks, but if you cannot define what makes you happy, then we might just miss the target. Remember the thought that enthusiasm and dedication is infectious? I have found one thing in common amongst the mentors in my life and the people I personally know and regard as successful people. They bring an excitement and dedication to everything they do. They seem genuinely happy in their career path. From farmers, teachers, preachers, to corporate leaders and salespeople. Don't get me wrong, we all encounter the "Stupid Rules" that we should fight to remove, and we don't always like the circumstances around us. But if you stepped back and viewed their life as a whole, you would find that deep down, they loved what they did.

What parts of your career to you love? What parts of your job or career do you loathe? Are they essential or necessary functions? We spoke about aligning goals and building a team of allies. What frustrations of your daily life could you easily remove? What opportunities could you present to your team to take on a new challenge that would make them happier? Have you ever thought about it? Remember the 4th Quarter survey I administered to my team? In management, sometimes we lose sight of the quantity of busy work that has been created over the years (*my Algebra homework*). We simply keep pawning off menial tasks to our team members without giving a second thought to whether the task could be improved, amended or removed altogether. Don't miss the opportunity to have the discussion in that moment. If a small goal you've set for yourself is to increase your happiness (or simply remove a few minor frustrations), don't lose sight of the fact that you can align your minor goal to your team's goals on the same quest.

I love building marketing plans and designing marketing materials for myself and for companies. I love writing copy and "using my words" (as parents tell their children).  Others might loathe that particular task. I might be able to take that task off your plate to...*watch this*...help you achieve your goal. And at the same time, be able to achieve my similar goal of increasing my happiness as well.  I may not be the best at writing copy, but the risk is minimal when it will be reviewed before release anyway, right?  And besides, if you loathe the task and I can remove 90% of the task from your plate, we both win, right?

As you might have gathered, I am a big proponent of cross-training employees.  I have seen the smiles and general happiness it can create for those employees who want to grow within their job or career, want to learn new skills, or simply try something new — training production workers as forklift drivers, taking inside customer service reps outside of the office walls to meet with customers, allowing alternate team members to work on a new project. Every opportunity you can create for someone to shine brings new possibilities to be discovered.  These possibilities are precious. What small happiness opportunity would you like to be given a chance to try in your career? What small happiness opportunities can you create for your team?

What can I do as an employee? Volunteer for projects, ask to help, assist your coworkers when you can. Believe me, it gets noticed...

As we try to define if we are "Happy" or "Successful", try thinking along the lines of what are we happiest or most successful _doing_... You might surprise yourself when you discover your answer.

# Part 8:

# Food for Thought
# & Conclusion

---

We've covered a lot of ground in a short number of pages. I am hopeful that together we can turn "Who Made these Stupid Rules" into series of personal and corporate success stories of breaking down the needless barriers that hold us back, dim our view, or otherwise detour us from our ultimate goals. But in the meantime, I have a few final points and requests I would like to convey.

### *Baseline Questions Revisited:*

First, let's review the Baseline Questions for Thought from the beginning of the book.

1.) You are approaching an airport ticket counter. You are faced with the snaking rope line to compress dozens of people into a small area. There is no one in line in front of you... Do you:

A.) Skip the rope line completely and walk directly up to the ticket counter?
B.) Walk through the entire rope line and wait to be called at the "Stop Here for next opening" sign?
C.) *Have you ever thought about this before? Will you smirk to yourself the next time you encounter it?*

2.) You are entering a grocery or retail store. There are designated "Enter" and "Exit" doors, but both have automatic door-openers... Do you:

A.) Walk into the closest door, regardless of Enter / Exit signage?
B.) Walk only into the correct "Enter" door?
C.) *As you approach the door next time, will you smirk as you watch people go out of their way, counting their extra steps, to walk through the "Correct" door?*

3.) When calling a business and the call is answered by an automated phone menu... Do you:

A.) Immediately push "0" without listening to all of the options?
B.) Listen to all of the options before making your selection?
C.) *Will you quietly think to yourself about how the Personability of simply having a real person answer the phone has been lost nowadays?*

4.) When setting goals, do you tend to:

A.) Set a small goal you know is achievable?
B.) Set a large goal you think you have a very small chance of achieving?
C.) *Will you think about aligning some of your goals with people around you? And how you might help others achieve theirs?*

5.) Think about your greatest personal or business accomplishment. How was it achieved?

A.) By following the standard prescribed set of guidelines?
B.) By creating your own path?
C.) *Will you begin to think about other opportunities you might have uncovered along the way or highlight the opportunities that you may have found?*

6.) Would you call yourself Successful? Would you say that you're happy?

If you remember the way you answered to yourself in the beginning of the book, have any of your answers changed? If your overall answer hasn't changed, has your thought process for "how" you think about the answer changed? Or did you come up with completely new answers for yourself? *(If you did, please send them to me...I'd love to see the difference between your first thought and your final thoughts.)* Ok, for those of you who wrote these questions down at the beginning of the book, you might have noticed a small change. I'll admit that I added a 3$^{rd}$ option to the questions. Not in an attempt to tilt the scales in my favor, simply because I've stressed throughout this book the importance of looking for hidden possibilities. Just because I provided two answers in the beginning of the book, that doesn't mean that there are only two answers... or three...or four...or any limits at all...

## *Final Requests:*

This isn't like Algebra II... I promise that although there are no grades here, these final requests are not mere busy work. It's simply something for you to ponder and try. You might bring a smile to someone's face...and that's never a bad thing.

> *First Request* – When you finish this book, call, text or email two loved ones - a parent, grandparent, spouse, other family member, friend, or customer. Tell them that you've just read "Who Made these Stupid Rules" and ask them about one of their personal goals. Their goal(s) might surprise you, if you've never talked about goals before.
>
> Then, and here is the real part of the request, ask them how *you* might be able to help *them* achieve their goal. *You might be thinking to yourself, Adam...you're a moron. What if their goal is to take a vacation in Italy? Am I on the hook to help them pay for the trip?* No....calm down... Perhaps, one thing that is holding them back is something simple. Perhaps they simply need someone they trust to watch their dog or house while they are away. Perhaps they just want confirmation, from a loved one, that their goal isn't ridiculous. Perhaps a "Stupid Rule" is holding them back...but now you're armed with simple ways around "Stupid Rules", now aren't you?
>
> Perhaps, it is all about the finance or cost aspect of the trip itself. You might not be able to help with that, but if you didn't already know that they wanted to visit Italy, now you are armed with

motivational items to brighten their days in the mean time – like online pictures, magazine articles or stories, vacation planning info links, or even money saving tips or coupons. Those cost nothing but a little of your time, and might make the world of difference to them. *Remember the part in this book about making 2 Minutes last for Days?*

This might sound strange coming from someone who wrote a book about accomplishing goals, but sometimes the journey and exploration is the most enjoyable part. I think back to all of the times in my life that I've started a quest for one thing and ended up on a seemingly completely different path exploring newly-discovered opportunities. As you try to help others achieve their goals, you can create a special bond that is deeper than the mere casual connection. Personability....

*Second Request* – Once you've had the conversation with two of your loved ones, take the conversation to work. Tell a manager, coworker, or your team members that you've read this book and ask them about their goals. Ask them how you might help them achieve their goals. Use a Post-It Note *(you're welcome for the incredible sales explosion you will undoubtedly enjoy, 3M)*, and write down the goal to keep in your folder, on your desk or stuck to your office wall to help motivate you both to achieve their goal.

Someone might ask you what is written on the note. You can proudly tell them that you are trying to help someone achieve a goal. You never know when opportunity will knock on your door to give you the perfect outlet to help them achieve the goal. But posting it, will reinforce to both of you that you truly intend to help them with their goal. It might just start a conversation about a goal others might be willing to help you achieve.

*Third Request* – Send me your feedback on your own success stories. "Stupid Rules" you've been able to break through in your personal or business life. The things from this book that you've tried, how they worked, the progress so far, what you're working on currently and how people around you responded. Most importantly, the opportunities or hidden potential you might have uncovered. *(The website and contact information is at the very end of this book.)*

### **_Final Food for Thought:_**    *(Again with food...)*

I've had a tremendous amount of fun writing this book. I sincerely hope that you've had fun reading it and perhaps will tackle your next obstacle with a slightly different viewpoint. There were dozens of stories that I could not include in this book, some funny, some sad, but all learning experiences for me that I wish I would have had more opportunities to relay. Perhaps we can include them in the next book. But as we reach the conclusion, there are a few simple thoughts I would like to convey a final time, simply because they have guided me, meant so much to me, and I have been able to use them every day in my personal life and career to date.

1.) Again...my adopted personal motto:

An Employee only **_Values/Trusts/Respects_** the Company as much as they **_FEEL_** the Company **_Values/Trusts/Respects_** them.

I promise you that the more this thought is spoken, it can truly start changing the way you view and interact with those around you.

2.) The best job interview on earth is your current job. Whether you plan to stay at your company "forever" or are currently looking for a new employment opportunities, you will leave a lasting impression on your co-workers, managers, owners, and customers...never forget the customers. I cannot tell you how many of my customers and coworkers have asked to use me as a reference or advice when they have left to pursue other opportunities.

But more importantly than references or transitions, the skills and opportunities you can be afforded in your current company can provide the outlet for you to achieve your ultimate goals. When we all keep our eyes open, you never know what opportunity will be around the next corner.

3.) The new definition of *Personability*: The inherent desire to relate to people you know on a deeper level than that of a mere casual connection. A human trait, regardless of career path, age or walk of life, which instinctually draws in passersby with an almost magnetic pull, charismatic charm, and the subliminal knowledge that he/she truly cares for others' well-being.

Try to develop a deeper connection to those around you. Try to help them achieve their goals, try to brighten their days, try to align your goals, and most of all, try to never hold them back with the "Stupid Rules" of daily life.

*Make 2 minutes last for days, but try to make them good days...*

4.) Never forget that achieving a goal is not the finish line. It is simply part of the journey. Life continues, the quest for improvement continues, and your desire can continue long after achieving a major goal. Move on to the next goal... opportunities don't always wait for you.

5.) Every personality is different and that is not a bad thing. In fact, that's what makes us all special. Our backgrounds, experiences, our varying definitions of details and risk, and our outlook on the future. Include different people in the discussion, learn from each other, grow together. You never know who can be on the Team of Allies. Remember that regardless of the Type of Duck...***All Ducks can Fly***...

6.) Don't equate Fame with Success. Don't quash other's goals or judge them by your own set of goals. I'm sure that there were many people who tried to quash the automatic bread slicer initiative of 1928. *(Evil Bread Knife conglomerates strike again...)* Strive to improve every way we can. Discover what "Sliced Bread" moments might be waiting for us.

And because I am who I am….I will leave you all with a funny thought…

7.) Finally…don't worry about getting caught mumbling "that is such a Stupid Rule" to yourself in a business meeting in the future. Perhaps, this book will be so wildly popular, that you will start seeing "Let's Remove our Stupid Rules" from corporate propaganda posters in the coming years. If you want, I'll even design them for you…. For a small fee.

**Goal Ripple**

Submit your thoughts, experiences, comments 24 hours a day to GoalRipple.com.

*Coming soon from Adam M. Brest, a complete library of Sales Training, Team Motivation, and Goal Alignment tools and materials to help your business grow and inspire you to achieve your goals.*

*A Personal Thank You –*

I would like to extend a sincere thank you for everyone who made this book possible. To those special people in my life who may have rolled their eyes when I stepped on my soapbox, but have supported and guided me along this journey called "Life".

And to you, the reader, for allowing me into your lives for a brief time...and hopefully we will have more opportunities over the years to share a few more laughs and create opportunities for growth.


Sincerely,

Adam M. Brest